How to
Deal With Teachers
Who Are
Angry,
Troubled,
Exhausted, or
JUST PLAIN CONFUSED

*For Lola Malone. She has inspired me with
her humble heart, blessed me with her giving spirit,
and energized me with her optimistic outlook. She is the
wind beneath my wings.*

Elaine K. McEwan

How to
Deal With Teachers
Who Are
Angry,
Troubled,
Exhausted, or
JUST PLAIN CONFUSED

CORWIN PRESS
A SAGE Publications Company
Thousand Oaks, California

For information:

Corwin Press
A Sage Publications Company
2455 Teller Road
Thousand Oaks, California 91320
www.corwinpress.com

SAGE Publications Ltd
1 Oliver's Yard
55 City Road
London EC1Y 1SP
United Kingdom

Sage Publications India Pvt. Ltd.
B-42, Panchsheel Enclave
Post Box 4109
New Delhi 110 017 India

Printed in the United States of America

Library of Congress Cataloging-in-Publication Data

McEwan, Elaine K., 1941-
How to deal with teachers who are angry, troubled, exhausted, or just plain confused / Elaine K. McEwan.
    p. cm.
Includes bibliographical references and index.
ISBN 0-7619-3818-4 (cloth) — ISBN 0-7619-3819-2 (pbk.)
    1. School supervision. 2. Teacher-principal relationships. I. Title.
LB2806.4.M39 2005
  371.2′012—dc22

                                                   2004028777

This book is printed on acid-free paper.

05   06   07   08   09   10   9   8   7   6   5   4   3   2   1

Acquisitions Editor:	Robert D. Clouse
Editorial Assistant:	Jingle Vea
Production Editor:	Kristen Gibson
Copy Editor:	Marilyn Power Scott
Typesetter:	C&M Digitals (P) Ltd.
Proofreader:	Annette Pagliaro
Cover Designer:	Michael Dubowe

Contents

Preface

In a recent burst of spring-cleaning, I came upon a classroom observation journal from my days as an elementary school principal. The entry that caught my eye was scribbled in response to this question a teacher had written on the chalkboard: *How do you know if you've had a good day?* I had written on that long-ago day, "It's been a good day when I've been to every classroom to visit and I've connected with every teacher on a personal or professional level."

Underneath this statement I had briefly noted four interactions with teachers thus far that day:

- Listened to an angry staff member rant about moving to a smaller home with her newly retired husband (his idea)
- Conferenced with a troubled teacher who refused to provide her telephone number for the teacher "phone tree" lest she become the recipient of crank calls
- Encouraged an exhausted new mother just back from maternity leave who was frazzled over the demands of juggling sleepless nights and hyperactive first graders
- Explained the meaning of *cooperative* in cooperative learning to a confused teacher

After the list I had jotted down this observation: "Being a principal is such a fluid job. I never feel as though I'm doing enough. There's always one more classroom to visit, one more discussion to hold. How can I keep them all motivated?"

Dealing productively with problem teachers has always been a challenge for principals, but the stakes are much higher now.

In today's results-oriented educational world, even two ineffective teachers can cause your school and its students to be left behind. When accountability for achievement is high, all teachers must be as close to peak performers as possible. Your mission is to find creative, humane, supportive, timely, *and* tough ways to deal with teachers who, for whatever reasons, *aren't* producing.

WHO THIS BOOK IS FOR

I have written *How to Deal With Teachers Who Are Angry, Troubled, Exhausted, or Just Plain Confused* specifically for school principals who desire to become more skilled in dealing with difficult teachers toward the goal of maximizing student learning and achievement. Throughout this book, I speak frankly and practically to principals as a colleague and former principal. Having said that, however, the following audiences will also find the book to be helpful:

- Supervisors, mentors, or coaches whose goal is to encourage the principals with whom they work to become more confident and successful in their relationships with difficult teachers
- College and university teachers of courses in administration, supervision, or evaluation who wish to introduce prospective principals to the challenges of interacting positively with a diverse and difficult staff
- Central office administrators who are expected to deal personally with angry, troubled, exhausted, and confused teachers themselves, as well as supervise, coach, and mentor the principals in their districts
- Classroom teachers who are considering the principalship and wish to broaden their perspective regarding one of the most challenging aspects of moving from the classroom to the principalship—dealing with teachers who were once their colleagues and are now their challenges
- Department chairpersons who have supervision and evaluation responsibilities

- Classroom teachers who lead grade-level teams, serve on site councils, and chair study groups and task forces
- Literacy coaches who work with a broad range of teachers in efforts to raise student achievement
- Specialists (e.g., librarians; music, art, physical education, and reading teachers; psychologists; and special education resource teachers) who deal with large numbers of classroom teachers in their service and support roles

SPECIAL FEATURES OF THE BOOK

How to Deal With Teachers Who Are Angry, Troubled, Exhausted, or Just Plain Confused contains the following special features:

- Assertive intervention scripts that demonstrate how to talk with troublesome teachers about their problems—explicitly, systematically, and supportively
- Sixty ways to energize, empower, encourage, and motivate teachers
- Answers to the most-often asked questions from practicing principals about dealing with dysfunctional teachers
- Roundtable discussions with highly effective principals on the "big ideas" of each chapter
- Actual case studies detailing how highly effective principals have dealt with difficult teachers
- Two resource sections—The Communicator's A–Z Handbook, full of quips, quotes, and suggestions to improve your one-to-one interactions with trying teachers—and The Culture Builder's Toolkit, packed with process exercises and assessment tools to help you create and nurture a positive school culture

OVERVIEW OF THE CONTENTS

Chapter 1 describes seven habits of attitude and action that are essential for dealing effectively with dysfunctional teachers:

1. Being an assertive administrator

2. Being a character builder

3. Being a communicator

4. Nurturing a positive school culture

5. Being a contributor

6. Conducting assertive interventions

7. Doing it today

Chapter 2 describes the critical attributes of an *assertive intervention* (AI), a tool for dealing explicitly, supportively, and systematically with difficult teachers.

Chapter 3 examines angry teachers and offers ways to deal specifically with these most challenging of employees. Whether teachers' angry feelings are justified or imagined, short-term or deep-seated, passive-aggressive or out of control, evident to everyone or focused on just one or two individuals, this chapter will help you find the courage you need to reduce, if not eliminate, teacher hostility.

Chapter 4 focuses on the troubled teacher—whether temporarily because of life's ups and downs or more seriously due to a mental disorder. The troubled teacher's problems are usually multifaceted and may take various forms in the classrooms and hallways of your school. Learning how to build trust, suggest options, and offer support without being patronizing or invasive is a tricky endeavor. This chapter will suggest some ways that have worked for highly effective principals around the country.

Chapter 5 describes strategies for managing relationships with teachers who are exhausted, stressed, or just plain burned out. To deal effectively with teachers in this category, principals need to pay special attention to their own physical and mental health. "In order to change the behavior of others, first look at your own behavior" is the big idea of this chapter.

Chapter 6 will help you deal with teachers who range from confused to incompetent. If you have too many marginal teachers on your staff, you no doubt experience low achievement, inappropriate student behavior, disastrous parent-teacher relationships, and lack of collaboration among faculty members. This chapter provides suggestions for dealing with low-performing teachers as well as critical guidelines for keeping what you do within the confines of the contract and the limits of the law.

Chapter 7 suggests sixty ways to energize, empower, encourage, and motivate teachers. These ideas will help you deal positively with problem teachers, *and* they will encourage your star teachers to remain committed and productive.

As noted earlier, there are two resources at the end of the book that will make it a handy reference long after you finish reading it start to finish.

A MATTER OF DEFINITION

I use the following terms throughout the book to refer to all of the teachers in the universe who are problematic in some way: *dysfunctional, troublesome, difficult, challenging,* and *tough.* Some of them also define the situation that you, the principal, are in when faced with their behavior. Take heart, however. As you gain expertise, you will quickly graduate from merely *dealing* with difficult teachers to *helping, facilitating, supporting, empowering, energizing, motivating,* and *leading* them.

Although I only refer to certified staff throughout the book, many of the suggested approaches and scripts are applicable to custodians, secretaries, lunchroom supervisors, instructional aides, and any other job category you employ and supervise in your school. An angry custodian or abusive lunchroom supervisor can impact the culture and effectiveness of a school as powerfully as a confused classroom teacher.

I use the terms *confront* and *confrontation* throughout the book. Although dictionary definitions of these terms sometimes include the concepts of defiance or antagonism, there is a third meaning that I wish to embrace exclusively: *acknowledging and meeting a problem teacher face to face with honesty, boldness, and confidence.* To confront teachers in the context of this book means making them aware in calm and forthright ways that you have observed their behaviors, are able to define them in detail, and are comfortable discussing them in rational ways. Furthermore, you are willing to lend support and resources if needed to address the problem, and you will not ignore further manifestations of the problem. Confrontations as described in the context of this book are never arrogant, hostile, or antagonistic.

Last, you may notice that only in rare instances do I use the singular form of the word *teacher*. This in no way implies that you have multiple faculty members in every category of difficult teachers. Rather, it enables me to avoid the clumsy repetition of the personal pronouns, *he* and *she*, making for smoother reading for you.

A CAUTIONARY NOTE

This book is not a legal document. It is intended to provide accurate information about subject matter. It is sold with the understanding that the publisher and the author are not engaged in rendering legal or other professional services. Specifically, the recommendations contained herein are guidelines only and not legal advice, and the publisher and the author do not warrant in any manner their suitability for any particular usage. If legal advice or other expert assistance is required, the services of an attorney or other competent professional, with knowledge of all laws pertaining to the reader and the jurisdiction, should be sought.

I am not implying that the recommendations of this book are the only methods or procedures for dealing with difficult teachers. The AI model is one of many tools you can use to deal with difficult teachers. Therefore, it is essential that you thoroughly review your district's evaluation procedures, negotiated contract, and policies before using any of the suggestions in this book.

ACKNOWLEDGMENTS

Highly effective administrators from around the country contributed the case studies, anecdotes, and reflections you will find throughout the book. I am grateful to each of them for their careful completion of a lengthy questionnaire and for the time they also gave for further follow-up conversations and e-mails in many cases. Their names are listed alphabetically here: Sandra Ahola, Jan Antrim, Corinne Archie-Edwards, Carol Blades, Lynn Blair-Thompson, Sue Braithwaite, Ron Collins, Dee Condon, Kathie Dobberteen, Laurence Fieber, Mark Frankel, Mary Kay Gallagher, Margaret Garcia-Dugan, Elsie Heller, C. J. Huff, Kathy Johnson, Shirley Johnson, Paula Kindrick-Hartsfield, Todd Lambert, Lola Malone, Nancy Moga, Phyllis O'Connell, Doug Pierson, Jim Ratledge, Kathy Schneiter, Craig Spiers, Cathie West, Dean Wharton, Todd White, Joseph Wyatt, and Lydia Zuidema. Where appropriate, I have cited their contributions in the book, but in many instances their input remains anonymous.

Special thanks to the following teachers who shared their personal perceptions of what teachers need in order to be positive and productive contributors in their schools: Susan Latin, Kristen MacKay, Janice Palfenier, and Dana St. John.

I am especially grateful to my brother, Dr. Larry Lantinga, and his partner, Dr. Mary Schohn, for their helpful comments and suggestions regarding motivational interviewing in Chapter 2 and mental disorders in Chapter 4.

Anne Lamott (1995) says that writing a book is like putting an octopus to bed (p. 94). I agree. Just when you think you have all of the arms tucked safely under the covers, one of them slips out and starts flapping. I am especially grateful to my copy editor, Marilyn Power Scott, who helped me to put this "octopus to bed." She is a gracious woman with a wonderful sense of humor who is also a dream of a copy editor. She improves every manuscript with a deft and subtle hand. To date, although we have never met in person, we have worked together on half a dozen books. It's never easy to submit to the discipline of copyediting, but Marilyn always makes it a lovely and growth-evoking experience. Thank you, Marilyn.

As always, I owe a special debt of gratitude to my husband and business partner, E. Raymond Adkins. Those readers who have attended my workshops and presentations know what a steady and supportive presence he is. His wisdom and common sense are the final arbiters of what goes into all of my books.

Corwin Press gratefully acknowledges the contributions of the following people:

Sue Segura
Principal
Fernley High School
Fernley, NV

David Brom
Principal
Champlin Park High School
Anoka-Hennepin I. S. D. #11
Champlin, MN

Tyrone Olverson
Principal
Lincoln Heights
  Elementary School
Lincoln Heights, OH

Joseph Staub
Resource Specialist Teacher
Thomas Starr Middle School
Los Angeles, CA

Patti J. Larche
Director of Curriculum and
  Instruction
Phelps-Clifton Springs CSD
Clifton Springs, NY

Carla Fry
Principal
Woodlands Elementary School
Ponca City, OK

Steve Hegner
Principal
Brady Middle School
Pepper Pike, OH

Scott Hollinger
Principal
McAuliffe Elementary School
McAllen, TX

Michelle M. Pecina
Principal
James Monroe Year-Round
  Elementary School
Madera, CA

About the Author

 **Elaine K. McEwan** is a partner and educational consultant with The McEwan-Adkins Group, offering workshops in instructional leadership, team building, and raising student achievement, K–12. A former teacher, librarian, principal, and assistant superintendent for instruction in a suburban Chicago school district, she is the author of more than thirty-five books for parents and educators. Her Corwin Press titles include *Leading Your Team to Excellence: Making Quality Decisions* (1997), *Seven Steps to Effective Instructional Leadership* (1998), *The Principal's Guide to Attention Deficit Hyperactivity Disorder* (1998), *The Principal's Guide to Raising Reading Achievement* (1998), *Counseling Tips for Elementary School Principals* (1999) with Jeffrey A. Kottler, *Managing Unmanageable Students: Practical Solutions for Educators* (2000) with Mary Damer, *The Principal's Guide to Raising Math Achievement* (2000), *Raising Reading Achievement in Middle and High Schools: Five Simple-to-Follow Strategies for Principals* (2001), *Ten Traits of Highly Effective Teachers: How to Hire, Mentor, and Coach Successful Teachers* (2001), *Teach Them ALL to Read: Catching the Kids Who Fall through the Cracks* (2002), *7 Steps to Effective Instructional Leadership, Second Edition* (2003), *Making Sense of Research: What's Good, What's Not, and How to Tell the Difference* (2003) with Patrick J. McEwan, *Ten Traits of Highly Effective Principals: From Good to Great Performance* (2003), and *Seven Strategies of Highly Effective Readers: Using Cognitive Research to Boost K–8 Achievement* (2004). *How to Deal With Parents Who Are Angry, Troubled, Afraid, or Just Plain Crazy, Second Edition* (2004).

Elaine was honored by the Illinois Principals Association as an outstanding instructional leader, by the Illinois State Board of Education with an Award of Excellence in the Those Who Excel Program, and by the National Association of Elementary School Principals as the National Distinguished Principal from Illinois for 1991. She received her undergraduate degree in education from Wheaton College and advanced degrees in library science (MA) and educational administration (EdD) from Northern Illinois University. She lives with her husband and business partner, E. Raymond Adkins, in Oro Valley, Arizona. Visit Elaine's Web site at www.elainemcewan.com where you can learn more about her writing and workshops and enroll in online seminars based on her books, or contact her directly at emcewan@elainemcewan.com.

Seven Habits of Highly Effective Principals

How to Deal With Difficult Teachers

Before you get started . . .

Compare your own experience to that of this principal:

Angry, troubled, exhausted, and confused teachers do more to impact morale and school climate than anything. After a while, other teachers become tired of hearing the complaining and begin to distance themselves from them. Consequently, the staff loses some of its desire to collaborate and work as a team. This creates fragmentation which, in turn, impacts school improvement initiatives.

—C. J. Huff

Several years ago, I purchased a term life insurance policy. Although no physical exam was required, I did have to answer a series of questions over the telephone. The first question on the list was "What day is it?" I answered the question correctly, but asked the interviewer why it was necessary. "To see if you're in touch with reality," she replied. Management consultant Carl

Frost of the Scanlon Leadership Network (2003) is well known for asking the same question of his corporate clients to remind them to stay alert regarding what's happening in their organizations. "Wake up and face reality," is his message. Difficult teachers are the reality that many administrators are currently ignoring in their schools.

Troublesome teachers are the proverbial "elephant" in faculty meetings. *Everyone* knows the elephant is there, but few are willing to confront the beast for fear of getting trampled. Many low-performing schools (and even some seemingly successful ones) are overrun with elephants. When the herd comes thundering down the hallway, everyone disappears, including, in some cases, the principal. It's time to wake up and face these enormous beasts. If you don't, your school may fail and take you along with it.

Before you can deal productively with difficult teachers, you must first examine your own attitudes and behaviors—the things you habitually think, say, and do. Dealing with difficult teachers demands that you face your own character flaws before you tackle those of your teachers. In fact, some teachers have suggested that my next book should be titled *How to Deal With Principals Who Are Angry, Troubled, Exhausted, or Just Plain Confused.* (Note: For a comprehensive treatise on the topic of principal mistreatment of teachers, see Blase & Blase, 2003.)

We all make mistakes from time to time. I have certainly made my share of them—especially as a brand-new administrator. Thankfully, there were effective and caring teachers on my staff who pointed out what I needed to do differently. I listened to them, albeit with some frustration, and eventually became a strong instructional leader. In the beginning, I was impatient to bring about change. I had to learn to listen and wait—postures that did not come easily to me.

However, there were problems that couldn't wait. There were several dysfunctional teachers whose problems were long overdue for remediation. With the support of

> Leadership is worth the risk because the goals extend beyond material gain or personal advancement.
> By making the lives of people around you better, leadership provides meaning in life. It creates purpose.
>
> —*Heifetz and Linsky*
> *(2002, pp. 2–3)*

the superintendent, the district's legal counsel, and eventually the school board and teacher's union, I was able to address those issues, not always at the speed I desired, but with solid documentation and respect for due process. While teachers *do* have rights, they do not include the license to sexually, physically, verbally, and educationally abuse students. Some of the teachers in my school, those whose skills were the shakiest, believed that I was out to eliminate the *entire* faculty. There was uncertainty and even fear, but the effective teachers eventually came out from behind closed doors to embrace both shared leadership and their new principal. They began to see that our goal to raise achievement would only be realized when we were united in our expectations and values.

SEVEN HABITS FOR DEALING POSITIVELY WITH DIFFICULT TEACHERS

Whether your goal is to take the lead in reforming a dysfunctional school community or to deal with one or two difficult teachers, put the following seven habits of attitude and action into daily practice:

1. Being an assertive administrator

2. Being a character builder

3. Being a communicator

4. Nurturing a positive school culture

5. Being a contributor

6. Conducting assertive interventions

7. Doing it today

Each of these habits is essential to dealing with difficult teachers and, if practiced daily, will strengthen and enhance your instructional leadership.

Habit 1: Being an Assertive Administrator

Assertiveness is a mindset that impacts the way you communicate (words and body language) and behave (deeds) in your everyday (habitual) interactions with teachers. It is a positive, forthright approach to leadership that stands in stark contrast to less effective leadership styles characterized by either aggressiveness or hesitancy.

> **The most effective way to deal with students is also the most effective way to deal with teachers. Let your expectations be known to all—early on—and in all of your dealings with difficult teachers be firm, fair, and consistent.**
>
> **—Principal Craig Spiers**

Assertive administrators are (a) mature and self-defined, (b) unwilling to take personal responsibility for the difficulties of dysfunctional teachers, and (c) not readily distracted from the school's mission by teachers' inappropriate behaviors. They are able to set boundaries and differentiate themselves from teachers. Here are the capacities of self-differentiated administrators that set them apart from their aggressive and weak colleagues:

- The capacity to view oneself separately from teachers, with a minimum amount of anxiety about their feelings and problems
- The ability to maintain a nonanxious presence, present and attuned to what is happening now without worrying about tomorrow, when working with and interacting with teachers who are angry, troubled, exhausted, or confused
- The maturity to chart one's own course by means of an internal set of personal values rather than continually trying to figure out what others are thinking or trying to see which way "the wind is blowing" before making a decision
- The wisdom to be clear and committed about one's personal values and goals
- The willingness to take responsibility for one's own emotional being and destiny rather than blaming either others or uncontrollable cultural, gender, or environmental variables (adapted from Friedman, 1991, pp. 134-170).

In contrast to their assertive colleagues, aggressive principals revel in the power that comes from being in charge. They specialize in humiliating and demoralizing teachers, often in cruel and irrational ways (Blase & Blase, 2003; Carey, 2004). Aggressive administrators are bullies who, even though they already have position and evaluation power, seek to further dominate their subordinates. They foster anger, emotional stress, depression, and confusion.

> Because I keep difficult teachers in perspective, their impact on me is minimal. Their behavior often says more about them than me. Over the years I have learned to differentiate between our separate roles.
>
> —*Principal Laurence Fieber*

Hesitant principals, on the other hand, are fair game for angry, troubled, exhausted, and confused teachers. Under the "leadership" of a weak administrator, a critical mass of difficult teachers can easily take over a school, turning it into an unhealthy environment faster than you can say, "Change in working conditions." Weak or tentative principals are secretly troubled by the way teachers take advantage of them, but they are usually powerless to stand up either for themselves or for effective staff members who struggle in vain to maintain a positive school culture. They are unable to differentiate themselves from difficult teachers and often assimilate their anxiety and anger.

To determine if you have what it takes to be an assertive administrator, complete the Assertive Administrator Self-Assessment, Form 1.1. Further information and scoring directions can be found in The Culture Builder's Toolkit (Resource B). To become a self-differentiated, assertive administrator requires persistent attention to the remaining six habits. Friedman (1991) describes the journey to assertiveness or self-differentiation as "a lifelong process [the development of a habit] of striving to keep one's being in balance through the reciprocal external and internal processes of self-definition and self-regulation" (p. 134).

Habit 2: Being a Character Builder

Dealing with difficult teachers is a central responsibility of instructional leaders. To do it effectively, you must first commit to being a character builder: *a role model whose values, words, and deeds are marked by trustworthiness, integrity, authenticity, respect, generosity, and humility.* Pritchett and Pound (1993) advise, "You will find no better way to coach employees on what the new culture must look like than by how you carry yourself" (p. 79).

Form 1.1   The Assertive Administrator Self-Assessment

	Never	Seldom	Sometimes	Usually	Always
Indicator 1	1	2	3	4	5

I protect and honor my own rights as an individual and also protect the rights of others.

	Never	Seldom	Sometimes	Usually	Always
Indicator 2	1	2	3	4	5

I recognize the importance of boundaries and am able to stay connected to others while at the same time maintaining a sense of self and individuality.

	Never	Seldom	Sometimes	Usually	Always
Indicator 3	1	2	3	4	5

I have positive feelings regarding myself and am thus able to create positive feelings in staff.

	Never	Seldom	Sometimes	Usually	Always
Indicator 4	1	2	3	4	5

I am willing to take risks but recognize that mistakes and failures are part of the learning process.

	Never	Seldom	Sometimes	Usually	Always
Indicator 5	1	2	3	4	5

I am able to acknowledge and learn from my successes as well as my failures.

	Never	Seldom	Sometimes	Usually	Always
Indicator 6	1	2	3	4	5

I am able to give and receive both compliments and constructive criticism to and from staff.

	Never	Seldom	Sometimes	Usually	Always
Indicator 7	1	2	3	4	5

I make realistic promises and commitments to staff and am able to keep them.

Indicator 8   1   2   3   4   5

I genuinely respect the ideas and feelings of others.

Indicator 9   1   2   3   4   5

I am willing to compromise and negotiate with staff and others in good faith.

Indicator 10   1   2   3   4   5

I am capable of saying no to teachers and sticking to a position, but I do not need to have my own way at all costs.

Indicator 11   1   2   3   4   5

I can handle anger, hostility, put-downs, and lies from staff without undue distress, recognizing that I am defined from within.

Indicator 12   1   2   3   4   5

I can handle anger, hostility, put-downs, and lies from staff without responding in kind.

Indicator 13   1   2   3   4   5

I am aware of my personal emotions (e.g., anger, anxiety), can name them, and manage them in myself.

Indicator 14   1   2   3   4   5

I am prepared for and can cope with the pain that is a normal part of leading a school.

For helpful guidelines regarding how character builders conduct themselves during stress-filled confrontations with tough teachers, consult Figure 1.1, the Ten Commandments for Dealing With Difficult Teachers. These imperatives are succinct reminders that dealing with angry, troubled, exhausted, and confused teachers requires these character traits: *trustworthiness, integrity, authenticity, respect, generosity, and humility.*

Figure 1.1   Ten Commandments for Dealing With Difficult Teachers

    I. Thou shalt treat all teachers with dignity and respect, regardless of their personal or professional problems.

    II. Thou shalt not harass, threaten, intimidate, or humiliate teachers either in private or public.

    III. Thou shalt document all actions, discussions, and confrontations with teachers clearly and accurately.

    IV. Thou shalt give explicit, direct, and honest feedback to teachers in a quiet, calm, and confident way.

    V. Thou shalt not share information about teachers unless the conversations occur with the superintendent, the district's legal counsel, or the board of education in a closed session.

    VI. Thou shalt provide clear and definitive expectations in any directives or requests to teachers.

    VII. Thou shalt never subject teachers to the silent treatment or attempt to isolate them from the life of the school.

    VIII. Thou shalt make all decisions regarding teachers based on the best interests of the students, the mission of the school, and the welfare of the entire school community.

    IX. Thou shalt never become defensive with teachers.

    X. Thou shalt never become aggressive or hostile to teachers.

Character builders do more than model the enumerated character traits. They also *proactively* build character through the communication of high expectations to their teachers. Cathie West, principal of Mountain Way Elementary School in Washington state, has led several schools during her twenty-six years in the principalship. Early in her tenure at a new school, she enlists the teachers in a consensus-building process to develop a code of ethics unique to that building. According to Cathie, the process as well as the code that is created serves several purposes:

> Developing a code of ethics with a new faculty is a quick way to find out how teachers are really getting along. The process itself is very illuminating. Staff members feel safe in small groups to say what they really think, and during the exercise I listen to their conversations. It is especially helpful to hear staff members discuss why one code statement is important (e.g., "we need to say that everyone is valuable because classified staff have been treated unequally in the past") or why another item needs strengthening (e.g., "we need to include 'respecting teaching styles' because the previous principal had 'favorites'"). At Mountain Way School, for example, I learned that major curriculum decisions had been made from the top down, so teachers very much wanted a statement in the code about being consulted before changes were made in the school.

Cathie uses the information she acquires during the process to make changes that nurture a positive culture. Once the code is in place, she uses it to reinforce expectations at the beginning of each school year and to periodically remind teachers of their professional obligations to colleagues. The existence of a code of ethics, developed jointly with the staff, has been helpful in other instances as well. She explains:

> When I had to nonrenew a probationary teacher for professional misconduct, the code of ethics became a valuable tool at a meeting with the union reps. One look at the code and it

was clear that the teacher knew better than to engage in the behavior that she did.

The Culture Builder's Toolkit, found in Resource B, contains a process exercise to develop a code of ethics tailored to the culture of *your* school using Cathie's code as a model.

Habit 3: Being a Communicator

A communicator is a genuine and open human being with the capacity to listen, empathize, interact, and connect with teachers in productive, helping, and healing ways. If you have strong communication skills and are able to fulfill the demands set forth in this definition with confidence and success, proceed to Habit 4. If you need a refresher or want to enhance some specific aspect of communication, however, refer to The Communicator's A–Z Handbook in Resource A. It provides a comprehensive look at a wide range of verbal and nonverbal communication skills.

When it comes to working with difficult teachers, the key word in the definition is *productive.* While there are many instances in which you will counsel teachers, interacting in healing and helping ways with them, as a communicator you should *never* attempt treatment, therapy, or even casual counseling for emotionally or mentally troubled teachers. The counseling role can be misunderstood and easily abused by administrators. Here's a brief example from my own personal experience:

I once worked for a principal whose office was the headquarters for more than half a dozen angry, troubled, exhausted, and confused members of a very large staff. He gathered these dysfunctional folks unto himself like a mother hen, making their problems his own and encouraging them to share intimate details of their lives. This principal could be seen for hours before and after school in earnest conversations with these troubled teachers. On the other hand, if you weren't a difficult teacher, he didn't have time for you.

The wise principal is sensitive regarding the point at which a relationship with a teacher may be crossing the line from a mutual exchange of ideas and healthy discussion to an unhealthy dependency of the difficult teacher on the principal *or* vice versa. The principal's helping skills should be used to communicate expectations, offer support, suggest options, and provide instructional resources, but never to "fix" dysfunctional teachers. [For further discussion and description of communicators, see McEwan, 2003, pp. 1–20].

Principals' Roundtable: The Secret to Success

Elaine: You have all been successful in reducing, if not eliminating, the problems posed by angry, troubled, exhausted, or confused teachers. What's the secret to your success?

Judy Marquardt: We have worked very hard to build a professional learning community, using a collaborative approach to establish our mission and vision and then setting school improvement goals. The result is a cohesive staff with strong connections to our school and to each other that has reduced the number of negative staff members. Another by-product of collaboration is that our culture doesn't support negative teachers, so truly negative teachers tend to leave the school.

Todd Lambert: I believe that our students, the attitudes of parents, and leadership at both the building and district levels all play a significant role in how few difficult teachers we have.

Jim Ratledge: I credit an improved selection process that includes a thorough preselection screening for the fact that we have so few teachers with problems. The number of problem teachers in all categories was significantly reduced when a new superintendent gave principals authority to hire staff. At that point I was able to make huge improvements in the quality of staff.

Laurence Fieber: Due to a meticulous hiring process, unwavering support from me, and very high expectations that require stamina and hard work from teachers, we have almost no difficult teachers. With sixty-five staff members, I spend a considerable amount of time hiring competent people.

Kathie Dobberteen: Our district generally attracts and hires very good teachers, and it provides outstanding support for them during their first several years. However, it also has an aggressive policy of not re-electing temporary or probationary teachers if they are unable to measure up to our standards despite this assistance. The district also lends a great deal of support to principals when it is necessary to let people go.

Lydia Zuidema: I'm in a private school, and our teachers have a deep sense of commitment to their calling. I strive to provide order, stability, and assistance for them. I value them and their contributions highly, and so do parents. This makes for a very satisfied and productive staff.

Carol Kottwitz: Parents definitely play a role in reducing the number of ineffective teachers in my school as well. My parent community does not stand for ineffective teachers and so the administration works to weed out inefficiency. Also, my staff does a pretty good job of collaborating, and they alienate poor teachers to the extent that they eventually leave the building.

Margaret Garcia-Dugan: I had so few ineffective teachers (when I was a principal) because I did not tolerate them. A principal needs to be in control of the environment of the school just like the teacher needs to be in control of the classroom environment. I always tackled problems head-on. But the most important thing I did was to hire quality teachers. I think that is the single most important task of a principal. To have a great school, you need the best teachers. I believe if you work really hard on teacher selection, you will have fewer problems in the end.

Elaine: How did you find the best teachers?

Margaret Garcia-Dugan: I had a lengthy interviewing process for teachers to undergo. I made extensive reference checks prior to employment, and teachers also had to demonstrate their instructional expertise by teaching a ten-minute lesson. I asked questions that revealed their philosophies of teaching as well as their personal beliefs.

Elaine: Together you have painted a very complete picture of the things that highly effective principals do to reduce, if not eliminate, difficult teachers: (a) build a strong and positive culture, (b) maintain high expectations, (c) find and hire the right people, and (d) be willing to let people go right away if they don't measure up.

Habit 4: Nurturing a Positive School Culture

Culture consists of *the norms and expectations for how things are done and how people act in an organization.* When you become a principal, either for the first time or in a brand-new school, immediately begin to assess the cultural norms in your school. In addition, pay attention to its climate, *how members of the school community feel about the current status of a specific cultural norm.* Use both formal assessments, such as those provided in The Culture Builder's Toolbox in Resource B, and informal observation regarding what goes on in the office, hallways, classrooms, and teachers' work room. Once you have completed your assessment, it's up to you to begin working to change the cultural norms that negatively impact the achievement of the mission. Here's an example:

One aspect of school culture concerns how decisions are made—whether dictatorially, in a shared fashion, or somewhere in between. Teachers may feel comfortable about leaving decisions up to their principal if things are going well, if the staff has worked together for a long time, and if the principal always makes decisions in the best interests of the teachers. On the other hand, if a new principal comes along and tries to make decisions *without* consulting the faculty, teachers may suddenly become distrustful—especially if the new principal's decisions change their workload. The climate will change overnight.

Recall what Cathie West discovered while developing a code of ethics in her current school. Her teachers didn't like the fact that they had no role in reviewing or giving feedback to committees after decisions were made, the cultural norm before she was hired. Cathie was able to add some steps to the decision-making process, thereby changing the norm. This change in how decisions were made ultimately improved the climate in the building as generated by how teachers felt.

A major aspect of *your* school's current culture concerns how you deal with teachers whose behaviors undermine the school's effectiveness and productivity. For example, if I were to poll your faculty on this issue, they would undoubtedly be able to describe exactly what you do. *They* know whether you typically yell at a difficult teacher and then, once your anger has passed, forget about the problem. Or they might describe your policy as "don't ask, don't tell." Conversely, they might report that you deal directly and fairly with all staff members using a set of expectations and standards for professional behavior to which everyone is held accountable. However, if you are unwilling to confront incompetence or a lack of commitment to the school's mission among even a few faculty members, you will pay the price in the following ways:

- Lowered teacher morale
- The devaluation of the school's effective teachers
- Loss of trust and respect from parents and students—for you individually as well as your school
- Loss of teacher efficacy and empowerment
- A downward spiral of academic achievement and an upward spiral of behavioral problems

Turning around a negative or dysfunctional school culture requires that you pay scrupulous attention to your deeds (Habit 2) and words (Habit 3). Everything you do and say should be rooted to the greatest extent possible in a *strong and viable vision based on achievement, character, personal responsibility, and accountability for all of the members of the school community.*

> **There is no more powerful engine driving an organization toward excellence and long-range success than an attractive, worthwhile, and achievable vision of the future, widely shared.**
>
> —*Nanus (1992, p. 3)*

The challenge is that school culture is never static. Changes in personnel, circumstances, and district policies occur constantly, and even the smallest changes have the potential to chip away at a school's culture. To nurture a positive culture, you will want to regularly assess the health of your school. The sixteen indicators shown in Figure 1.2, The Healthy School Checklist, describe a healthy school. A scale of descriptors for each indicator as well as directions for scoring and interpreting the checklist can be found in Resource B. Once you have determined the "health" of your school, use the findings to develop suitable action plans.

Figure 1.2   The Healthy School Checklist

Indicator 1: All students are treated with respect by all staff members, to include principal, teachers, instructional aides, secretary and office staff, custodial staff, bus drivers, and cafeteria workers.

Indicator 2: The principal and staff establish high expectations for student achievement, which are directly communicated to students and parents.

Indicator 3: The principal and staff members serve as advocates for students and communicate with them regarding aspects of their school life.

Indicator 4: The principal encourages open communication among staff members and parents and maintains respect for differences of opinion.

Indicator 5: The principal demonstrates concern and openness in the consideration of teacher, parent, or student problems and participates in the resolution of such problems when appropriate.

Indicator 6: The principal models appropriate human relations skills.

Indicator 7: The principal develops and maintains high morale.

Indicator 8: The principal systematically collects and responds to staff, parent, and student concerns.

Indicator 9: The principal appropriately acknowledges the meaningful achievements of others.

Indicator 10: All staff members, classified and certified, are able to communicate openly with one another and say how they feel.

Indicator 11: The individual abilities, knowledge, and experience of all staff members are fully used.

Indicator 12: Conflict between various individuals (teachers, parents, students) is resolved openly and effectively, and there is a genuine feeling of respect for one another among these groups.

Indicator 13: The entire school community can articulate and is committed to the vision and mission of the school.

Indicator 14: Staff members can express their views openly without fear of ridicule or retaliation and permit others to do the same.

Indicator 15: Staff members can get help from one another and give help without being concerned about hidden agendas.

Indicator 16: The school climate is characterized by openness and respect for individual differences.

Habit 5: Being a Contributor

To foster your teachers' feelings of satisfaction and productivity pay attention to their needs: Be a contributor. A contributor *is a servant-leader, encourager, and enabler whose utmost priority is making a contribution to the success of others.* "If there is a single tool a principal should have, it is a mirror. Looking in that mirror, the principal can find the person who more than any other is both responsible for and accountable for the feelings of satisfaction and productivity among staff, students, and patrons. (Kelly, 1980, p. 53)

What do teachers need in order to be productive and satisfied employees? Money, benefits, and job security are certainly high priorities. In reality, if money and benefits were the *only* prerequisites for creating a productive teaching force, our vast urban school districts would be posting achievement gains that are off the charts. While making a living *is* essential, teachers need more than generous paychecks to become peak performers, especially given the current demands of teaching. (See the case study on exhausted teachers in Chapter 5.)

> Get the right people on board, confront the brutal facts, and establish a culture of discipline in which doing the right thing is built into the culture.
>
> —*Collins (2001, p. 88)*

When Lola Malone, principal of John Tyson Elementary School in Alabama, was asked to mentor new principals in her district, she thought carefully about what advice she could give them that would *guarantee* their success as leaders. She drew on her experience as a "contributor," a principal who is willing to provide what teachers need to be effective. The list that Lola passes on to her new administrative colleagues is shown in Figure 1.3. When the needs in this list are met, teachers can devote themselves to achieving the school's mission with minds, bodies, and spirits that are free of anger, distress, depression, exhaustion, and confusion.

> Consideration of others—an ethic of caring—is fundamental to moral leadership.
>
> —*Blase & Kirby (2000, p. 116)*

Figure 1.3   The Needs of Teachers: Lola's List

All teachers need to feel that their principals respect them as individuals and will protect their privacy.

All teachers need to know that their principals will deal with their problems directly and privately.

All teachers need to be given credit for their ideas, creativity, hard work, and willingness to take on additional responsibilities (both privately and publicly, both orally and in writing).

All teachers need to know that their principals will not jump to conclusions or make hasty decisions, particularly when their welfare is under consideration.

All teachers need principals who are available and listen to them.

All teachers need to have reasons and explanations given when plans derail, problems occur, requests cannot be fulfilled, or promises are broken.

All teachers need to have all of the information and facts put on the table and to be kept apprised of what is happening in their schools.

All teachers need to know that when possible and where appropriate, when decisions are made that affect them collectively or as individuals, they will be given opportunities for input and discussion.

All teachers need to know that their principals are fair and will not show favoritism to an individual or group.

All teachers need to know that their principals will keep open minds when they advance ideas or make suggestions for change.

All teachers need to know that they will be a part of the team when parent and student problems are under discussion, problems are being solved, or plans are being developed.

All teachers need to feel supported in their disciplinary decisions with students.

All teachers need to know that their principals will admit mistakes, sincerely apologize when wrong, and then move forward.

All teachers need to know that their principals will always send parents to them first if there are questions or concerns about what they are doing in their classrooms.

All teachers need to know they can bring problems and concerns regarding their principals' performance to the forefront and that such problems and concerns will be addressed honestly, immediately, and positively.

All teachers need to know that their principals value their personal lives and when appropriate and possible will take them into consideration when making requests.

If the concept of "serving" strikes you as contradictory to the assertive stance needed for dealing with problem teachers, you have confused it with "subservience." Your servant-leadership will enable teachers to be productive and successful in their work and also strengthen your influence as a leader. Nevertheless, in the short term, you may feel some resentment about "waiting on" staff members who are determined to undermine your leadership and even destroy your school. If so, I can relate. Fortunately, however, I learned very early in the principalship that looking out for Number 1 is a surefire way to destroy morale *and* self-destruct as a leader. If the needs listed in Figure 1.3 are *not* met (especially in the face of rising expectations and diminishing resources), a vicious cycle of anger, distress, exhaustion, and confusion sets in. Abused, disrespected, and demeaned subordinates often become the very angry, troubled, exhausted, and confused teachers that we later lament. [Note: For a more comprehensive description and discussion of contributors, see McEwan, 2003, pp. 151–162.]

> When I finally realized that one of the many hats I wear is that of "helper," I began having more success. I think teachers began to see that I was human and wanted to meet their needs. Not that I was 100% successful, but I made a lot more headway once their needs were met.
>
> —*Principal C. J. Huff*

Habit 6: Conducting Assertive Interventions

Habit 6 is focused on making teachers aware of behaviors that are standing in the way of *their* productivity in the classroom as well as the achievement of your schoolwide mission. Various terms have been used to describe honest, direct approaches to helping people confront inappropriate behaviors. They include, among others, "telling the truth in love" (Autry, 1991), "tough love" (Tough Love International, 2004), "fierce conversations" (Scott, 2002), and "motivational interviewing" (Miller & Rollnick, 2002).

Telling the truth in love requires courage and a moral commitment to confront reality. This down-home proverb cited by essayist

Barbara Kingsolver (1995) conveys a colorful mental picture: "If you never stepped on anybody's toes, you never been for a walk" (p. 45). To deal with dysfunctional teachers, you must "step on their toes." Susan Scott (2002) calls encounters in which we do this, "fierce conversations." She defines a fierce conversation thus: "one in which we come out from behind ourselves into the conversation and make it real" (p. 7). Often when we meet with difficult teachers, we end up talking too much and saying all the wrong things. We ask inane questions or sugarcoat the discussion with ill-advised compliments to avoid hurting teachers' feelings. We often don't get to the point or tell the truth. We babble all around the elephant in the middle of our office.

To help you confront the elephants in your school, I have packaged the applicable features of tough love, telling the truth in love, fierce conversations, and motivational interviewing into a systematic plan called an *assertive intervention* (AI). An AI is a communication tool to help you say what needs to be said to teachers who are angry, troubled, exhausted, or just plain confused, and to do it with truth, respectfulness, *and* confidence. Chapter 2 describes the characteristics of AIs and provides sample interventions as models.

> Courage isn't the absence of fear; it's proceeding in spite of it. Not holding back something you know needs to be said, telling the truth in the face of peril and pitfall. It's being candid when it may be dangerous. It's going ahead and doing it or saying it even if it's uncomfortable.
>
> —*Hawley (1993, p. 133)*

Habit 7: Doing It Today

One of my favorite columnists, now deceased, was Sydney Harris (n.d.) of the *Chicago Daily News.* He said, "Regret for the things we did can be tempered by time; it is regret for the things we did not do that is inconsolable."

There is never an "ideal" time to confront teachers who are behaving inappropriately, but if in doubt, do it today. Some have suggested that it is important to first earn the trust of teachers, proving that you care about them, before you attempt to confront them about inappropriate behavior. But I submit there are three crucial windows of opportunity for dealing with the most serious problems: (1) when you begin a new principalship, b) during the induction of newly hired or transferred teachers, or c) the moment a new problem arises or you notice a recurrence of a previous problem with any teacher.

Confronting fellow professionals, whether brand-new hires or teachers with decades of experience, can take its toll on your emotional, spiritual, and physical energy, to say nothing of the time it steals from nurturing positive aspects of your school's culture. But don't delay. I subscribe to the advice given by Pritchett and Pound (1993) in their small, but powerful book, *High–Velocity Culture Change: A Handbook for Managers*: "Start out fast and keep trying to pick up speed. *Leave skid marks*" (p. 43).

> It is often easier to avoid a problem than to feel an obligation to do something to solve it. As teachers we are trained to help students, but principals really need a different set of skills to work with adults so as not to make people feel that you are trying to change them.
>
> —*Principal Mark Frankel*

If nontenured teachers are behaving inappropriately, talk to them immediately. If you wait too long, they will conclude that you haven't noticed or don't care. One hopes that brand-new teachers have paid close attention to the expectations presented in your orientation as well as the code of conduct in the teacher handbook, but my rule of thumb is, "Assume nothing." I learned that lesson the hard way.

I vividly remember a closed session with the school board when they were deliberating over my recommendation to dismiss a probationary custodian. Among other notable deficiencies, he consistently "forgot" to shovel snow off the front walks. I had issued countless verbal reminders and written reprimands about the importance of attending to the requirements of his job description. However, one especially testy board member felt I hadn't been explicit enough. "Did you *specifically* tell him or put a statement *in writing* that spelled out that his failure to perform these tasks could result in his being fired?" he asked.

I had to admit that I hadn't put it quite that bluntly. "He's a probationary employee whose job is dependent on the quality of his work during the probation period," I gently argued. "Shouldn't he know that?" The board member was not buying it, and he convinced his colleagues that this employee deserved another chance. I learned a very important lesson during that meeting. Never assume that employees (whether custodians *or* teachers) know that their inappropriate behavior *can* result in unsatisfactory ratings, transfers to other schools, nonrenewal of contracts, or even dismissal proceedings. Lay it out in a brutally honest fashion if you sense that any of these possibilities might be forthcoming in the future.

If the behavior of experienced tenured employees suddenly becomes erratic, pay attention. The longer you neglect problem teachers, the guiltier you will feel every time you see them "doing it" again, thereby creating an additional problem—the deterioration of your own self-respect. Never make the mistake of thinking that your teachers' *personal* problems have nothing to do with their *professional* problems. "Well, he may be a chronic alcoholic, *but* he is a brilliant teacher." What about the student, parent, and staff complaints that are spilling out of his personnel file? Being a good teacher is far more than teaching a few lessons well. Don't fall into the trap of believing that confronting employees about inappropriate behavior constitutes meddling. Don't be paralyzed by the fear that your teachers won't like you if you confront them. You have a moral obligation to intervene. You were hired to fulfill a moral imperative; do it with character.

I was a brand-new principal, taking my first walk through the building. I began across the hall from my office in the classroom of a male, upper-grade teacher, John. He was seated behind his desk at the front of the room and had a male student on his lap. The students in the room seemed relaxed, and neither John nor the student looked embarrassed. I hurried to my office and called the superintendent to make an appointment as soon as possible.

I was angry. It was the kind of righteous anger one feels when a trust has been betrayed and a standard violated. Sergiovanni (2000) calls it "leadership by outrage," (p. 277). My meeting with the superintendent brought both good and bad news. The good news was that he would back my efforts to deal with this troubled teacher. The bad news was that I couldn't fire him the next day! The good news was that his inappropriate touching of students finally stopped—after three confrontations, each one escalating the stakes to a new level. The bad news was that in addition to being deeply troubled, John was also a terrible teacher. My mission was difficult, but not impossible. I had no choice but to accept it. I decided not to worry about the past. I had no control over it. I could only deal with the teacher today. So I did.

SUMMING UP

Dealing with dysfunctional teachers requires character, assertiveness, communication skills, a servant's heart, the support of a positive or improving school culture, and the courage to confront inappropriate behavior the first time it becomes evident. Your mission, and if you aspire to be a highly effective principal, you have no choice but to accept it, is to take on the challenge of dealing with teachers who are angry, troubled, exhausted, or just plain confused.

How to Conduct
an Assertive
Intervention

Tell It Like It Is

If you are like most principals around the country, you have one or more angry, troubled, exhausted, or just plain confused teachers in your school. And you are not alone if you feel guilty about having ignored them for too long or are depressed about the damage they are doing to the culture and achievement of your school. There is help just ahead, however. Whether you have an angry teacher who terrorizes colleagues, a troubled teacher who can't cope with classroom management, a burned-out teacher who is too tired to teach, or a confused teacher whose at-risk students continue to fail, you can stop feeling guilty or depressed by scheduling your first assertive intervention (AI) as soon as you finish reading this chapter.

An AI has several attributes that make it unique as a tool for dealing with difficult teachers: *It is an assertive, explicit, supportive, and systematic three-stage process intended to promote behavioral change in teachers.* We begin by discussing the critical attributes of AIs, describe each of their stages, consider some sample AIs, and show you how to conduct your first one.

THE CRITICAL ATTRIBUTES OF ASSERTIVE INTERVENTIONS

AIs Are Assertive

AIs are only as assertive as you are. As you will recall from our discussion in Chapter 1, assertive administrators are mature and self-defined individuals, unwilling to take personal responsibility for the difficulties of dysfunctional teachers, and refusing to be distracted from attaining their schools' missions. They lead from a sense of purpose grounded in strong values. Assertive administrators know that if they lower their expectations for even one teacher, they may delay or even derail the achievement of their school's mission.

AIs Are Explicit

AIs are explicit. They clearly describe the nature of what a teacher is doing and how the behavior negatively impacts the school community. The language used in Stage 1 of an AI is based on objective descriptions of behavior and avoids inflammatory adjectives that can cause defensiveness in the listener. For example, here are the opening statements I made during what I consider to be my very first AI, a confrontation with my upper-grade teacher described in Chapter 1:

John, I asked to meet with you today because I'm upset about the unacceptable behavior you exhibited in your classroom yesterday afternoon. You had a male student, Tom Justice, sitting on your lap. Your arms were wrapped around his body, hugging him, and his buttocks were pressed against your genitals. This inappropriate behavior reflects adversely on your reputation as a professional.

My heart was pounding when I opened my mouth, but I delivered this statement calmly. The teacher and I could have been talking about the weather or what we had for dinner. I did not, however, avoid the brutal facts of the case. When you speak in vague generalities or include positive statements to fill "air time," teachers can readily plead misunderstanding. AIs leave no room for confusion. If you can't describe inappropriate behavior directly to a teacher, no matter how personally distasteful or threatening that behavior may be to you, you will have a difficult time dealing with the teacher. (Note: When I confronted John more than two decades ago as a brand-new principal, I did so based on my instincts. Although the concept of a three-stage AI as described in this chapter has gradually evolved over the years, one critical attribute has not changed—the importance of confronting teachers directly and honestly. You may also wonder why I called my superintendent before calling the Department of Children and Family Services. More about that later.)

Q & A

Ella: Do AIs work with *every* difficult teacher?

Elaine: AIs are most effective when there is a solid reason to believe that teachers are ready, willing, and able to make changes in their behavior with strong support from you or in conjunction with professional help. For example, AIs don't work with incompetent teachers. Every interaction with these individuals must be carefully recorded, every observation must be scrupulously documented, and the entire process must follow all of the contractual and legal obligations in order to hold up in a due-process hearing. See the case study in Chapter 6.

AIs Are Supportive

Never conduct AIs without expressing your sincere intent to support teachers' efforts to eliminate problem behavior. Supportive services that might be offered, depending on the observed behaviors, include counseling (if available in your district), release time to visit exemplary teachers, the opportunity to work with an independent consultant, or the support of an in-district instructional specialist. Whether teachers accept and benefit from your support depends on their readiness, willingness, and ability to change.

In John's case, my support came in the form of ongoing monitoring. Here's what I said: "John, I'm going to be dropping in to your classroom at various times every day to remind you of how important it is to maintain professional behavior. Let me define 'professional behavior,' explicitly for you: It means that you don't touch any students, male or female, at any time, or in any way, or in any place, any more."

AIs Are Systematic

In addition to being explicit and supportive, an AI is also systematic. It is a sequential communication process consisting of three stages: (1) a sixty-second scripted *principal presentation,* (2) an untimed and open-ended period of teacher *reaction* or *response,* and (3) a joint principal-teacher *motivational exploration.* In the field of psychology, a process like this is called *directive,* not because you are telling the teacher what to do but because there is a definite structure to the discussion (Rollnick, Mason, & Butler, 1999, p. 31).

You can never be certain when you begin an AI how many of the three stages you will successfully complete in one meeting or even whether the eventual outcome will be a positive one. Those decisions are up to the teachers.

AIs Are Ongoing Processes

AIs are processes, not events. You don't do AIs, tell the teachers to change, and cross the problems off your list. The reality is that you cannot "make" teachers change their inappropriate behaviors with administrative mandates. Rather, you *conduct* AIs. The meaning of the verb *conduct* is to *show the way* or *lead,* more in the nature of a trail guide than a military general. You can only present teachers with options for improving their productivity and professionalism; they have to make conscious and intentional decisions to change. They must be "ready, willing, and able" (Miller & Rollnick, 2002, p. 10). Coming to the point of readiness to change may be relatively easy for someone who quit smoking in one day and hasn't picked up a cigarette in forty years. But behavioral change, even for mentally and emotionally healthy individuals, usually takes a significant amount of getting-ready time and occurs in a series of stages (Prochaska, Norcross, & Diclemente, 2002). For dysfunctional teachers, moving through these stages can take even longer. That is why an AI is a process, not an event.

Q & A

Ed: When is it appropriate to use AIs?

Elaine: It's appropriate to use AIs anytime you need to sit down with teachers and confront them honestly about inappropriate behavior. AIs aren't just for major problems. They are also appropriate formats for addressing minor issues with teachers. After hearing about AIs at a workshop, one principal used the format three times the following week:

(1) to talk with a teacher about the fact that his report card grades were unsupported by accurate formative testing data; (2) to confront a teacher about the amount of wasted time in his classroom; and (3) to model the AI format for the media specialist who was having a communication breakdown with her library assistant.

AIs Are Designed to Promote Teacher Change and Growth

An *instructional* intervention is an activity undertaken by a teacher to help a child who is failing. In the context of working with difficult teachers, an *assertive* intervention is an activity undertaken by a principal to help teachers who are failing to meet professional standards. The goal of AIs is to promote positive behavioral change. To sincerely promote teacher growth, you must communicate upfront your belief in teachers' abilities to change. If you initially confront teachers in a doubtful or accusatory spirit, you will fail. Goethe sums it up this way: "If you treat an individual as he is, he will stay as he is, but if you treat him as if he were what he ought to be and could be, he will become what he ought to be and could be."

For example, in my interactions with John, my deeply troubled teacher, I was never rude, demeaning, or unsupportive. After his inappropriate behavior ceased to be an issue, I focused on his marginal teaching and did everything in my power to help him become a professional teacher. I released him from his teaching responsibilities so he could visit classrooms in the school, district, and other districts. I allocated staff-development resources to hire an independent instructional coach to work with him and also provided release time in which he could plan lessons and work with his grade-level partner.

Actually, John wanted to become a more effective teacher. He genuinely tried to do what he was asked to do. He stopped touching his students inappropriately. He worked cooperatively with his coach. He treated me and his colleagues with respect. However, John was *unable* to think about and treat his students as learners.

He was unable to hold them accountable for turning in assignments, paying attention in class, or following classroom rules. He craved affirmation and affection from them and thus was unable to get results and achievement.

If teachers aren't ready, willing, or able to change after your first confrontation with them, your job is to keep confronting them until they make a decision to change. However, if they are unwilling or unable to change, even after lengthy supportive assistance, you have no choice but to invoke more stringent disciplinary measures and eventually initiate dismissal proceedings.

Teachers can decide to change for many reasons: (1) They respect the principal and the goals of the school and want to become a part of a winning team, (2) a critical mass of effective teachers is creating a positive culture of which they want to be a part, (3) their needs for acceptance, affirmation, and affiliation will be met by signing on to the school's mission, or (4) they are terrified of losing their jobs. In John's case, he liked being part of a school faculty, wanted to be accepted and affirmed, and was terrified of losing his job.

In the end, only you, with the support of your central office and school board, have the evaluative and position power necessary to provide motivation, support, options, incentives, and reasons (whether positive or negative) to lead teachers toward productive choices.

Q & A

Marlene: Does an AI require a culture change before it can be effective?

Elaine: An effective intervention is one that results in a teacher becoming a productive member of the team. You *can* conduct AIs in the absence of a positive culture, but the process is far more difficult for you. However, absent a positive school culture and given a couple of dozen dysfunctional teachers, you need to start somewhere!

THE THREE STAGES OF ASSERTIVE INTERVENTIONS

AIs have three distinct stages. On rare occasions, if a teacher is cooperative and ready to change, you might be able to move through all three stages in a single meeting. A more likely scenario, however, especially with difficult teachers, is to complete one stage per meeting. With some highly dysfunctional teachers, you will never get past the first stage.

The first two stages of the AI model have been inspired and informed by Scott's (2002) "fierce conversation." This model is used in the corporate world as a way to help executives and managers face reality in their organizations. Stage 3 adapts concepts and principles from Miller & Rollnick's (2002) motivational interviewing model, an approach widely used in psychotherapy.

Granted, schools are different from corporations, and teachers are not patients in therapy. But the key concepts of confronting reality and motivating people to change inappropriate behaviors are eminently applicable to the school setting.

Stage 1: Principal Presentation

The first stage of an AI is a meticulously planned and rehearsed sixty-second *principal presentation* that confronts teachers with their inappropriate behavior. Form 2.1 is a template on which to draft your statements in response to seven prompts. Exhibit 2.1 is a sample AI presentation to a high school teacher who has repeatedly been observed by students smoking in the boys' rest room, although smoking anywhere on campus is prohibited by district policy.

As you review the following seven prompts, also refer to the statements in Exhibit 2.1 made by Stan's principal regarding his inappropriate behavior. Consider how you might phrase your statements to a similarly difficult teacher.

1. Name and explicitly describe the behavior you want the teacher to eliminate. Focus on what the teacher is doing

Form 2.1   Assertive Intervention Planning Form

Name: Date:

Prompt	Principal's Statement
Behavior to be eliminated	
Explicit description of the behavior	
Principal's feelings about the behavior	
Explanation of how the behavior impacts the teacher	
Principal's personal contribution to the continuance of the behavior	
Principal's desire to resolve the issue	
Principal's invitation to the teacher to respond	

Exhibit 2.1 Assertive Intervention: Stan

Name: Stan   Date: October 23

Prompt	Principal's Statement
Behavior to be eliminated	Stan, I've asked to meet with you about the fact that you've been smoking in front of students in the boys' rest room on the fourth floor.
Explicit description of the behavior	Your violation of the no-smoking rule on school property is a serious violation of school board policies.
Principal's feelings about the behavior	I can't tell you how distressed I am by the fact that you're openly flouting school rules in front of students regarding something as addictive as nicotine.
Explanation of how the behavior impacts the teacher	Your behavior seriously damages your credibility as a role model for students, something that is taken very seriously by our board of education.
Principal's personal contribution to the continuance of the behavior	There have been rumors of your smoking on school grounds for several weeks, and I should have confronted you the first time I heard about it. But I chose to believe that it was a one-time error in judgment.
Principal's desire to resolve the issue	Stan, when we leave my office, I want to be assured that I won't ever have to talk to you about this problem again.
Principal's invitation to the teacher to respond	Tell me what your thinking is about this issue.

that *most* interferes with productivity and effectiveness. If you can't sum up the problem in one or two short statements, you are tackling too much at once.

2. Provide one or more specific examples of the behavior that you or others have observed, making sure that they adequately illustrate the impact the behavior is having.

3. Describe your personal feelings about what the teacher is doing (e.g., shocked, distressed, embarrassed, or disappointed).

4. Clarify what is at stake for the teacher if the behavior persists: Describe how it is affecting the teacher's reputation in the school and community, effectiveness in the classroom, students' achievement, or relationships with colleagues. If appropriate, mention the possible repercussion of a negative summative evaluation or a nonrenewal of contract.

5. Identify your contribution to this problem. If the problem is a persistent one and to date you have avoided confronting the individual, express regret that you have not done so sooner and offer a possible reason for the delay: (a) I expected you to recognize how destructive your inappropriate behavior is and deal with it yourself; (b) I thought your colleagues would confront you about how rudely you treat them in team meetings; or (c) I believed that when you read the letters of complaint from parents that I gave to you, they would serve as a wake-up call to change.

6. Strongly state your sincere desire to resolve the issue with speed, indicate your willingness to provide support and assistance, and include your expressed belief that eliminating the behavior will be an advantage to the teacher as well as to the school.

7. Invite the teacher to respond to what you have said.

When you have written a concise statement in response to each of the seven prompts, time the delivery of your presentation. It should take no more than sixty seconds. Once you have delivered your presentation to the teacher, an AI officially moves into Stage 2.

Stage 2: Teacher Response

Stage 2 is an open-ended and unstructured period of time during which teachers have the opportunity to react to your sixty-second presentation. Ideally they will make a statement acknowledging the existence of their problem and indicate a desire to work on and eliminate the unacceptable behavior. However, the typical difficult teacher is more likely to respond in one of the following ways: (1) refuse to say anything (i.e., sit in stony or bewildered silence), (2) deny the existence of the behavior (i.e., you're mistaken; I didn't do that); (3) refuse to recognize the behavior as detrimental to the school's mission or culture (what I did has nothing to do with me as a teacher); (4) state that other teachers do the same things and get away with them; (5) become angry and accuse you of harassment and unfairness, (6) threaten union intervention or lawsuits; or (7) blame uncontrollable circumstances, such as problems at home, illness, unsupportive colleagues, fuzzy expectations, uncooperative parents, lack of resources, or low-achieving and misbehaving students. Depending on whether your district requires a union representative to be present at any and all meetings, teachers may be advised to not respond at all and to wait until they see what you put in writing. Specific suggestions regarding how to react to these various types of teacher responses are found in the upcoming section titled "How to Conduct Assertive Interventions."

Mary Lou Casey (as quoted in Miller & Rollnick, 2002, p. 52) said it so well: "What people really need is a good listening to." Your role during Stage 2 is to listen attentively and thoughtfully to determine if the teacher is ready and willing to change. Once the teacher begins to talk, avoid any of the following responses that will inevitably derail a productive discussion (adapted from Miller & Rollnick, 2002, p. 50):

- Trying to persuade the teacher to do "the right thing"
- Asking closed-ended questions that shut down discussion
- Trying to make the teacher feel guilty or ashamed
- Labeling or diagnosing the teacher's behavior (e.g., alcoholic or depressed)
- Trying to identify what or who is to blame for the teacher's problem
- Being in too much of a hurry
- Taking the "I know what's best for you" position

Falling into these traps can readily sabotage the outcome of AIs. Review the presentation to Stan in Exhibit 2.1. Note that although the principal defines Stan's inappropriate behavior (smoking) and describes the consequences of his behavior for him and the school community (being an inappropriate role model and damaging his reputation), he does not take the "I'm going to make you do this or else" perspective.

If the teacher fails to acknowledge the existence of the behavior or seems unwilling at the time to do anything about it, your AI has not failed. The teacher just needs additional time and another AI presentation to realize two things: (1) You are serious in your intent to deal with the problem; and (2) there are benefits to be realized from making the change.

An AI is an ongoing process, and you have begun it. If the teacher responds positively and productively, the AI then moves into Stage 3, a dialogue or motivational conversation between you and the teacher in which you jointly explore ways to eliminate the behavior and develop an action plan.

Stage 3: Motivational Interview

During Stage 3, you and the teacher interact with the goal of developing a plan to eliminate the inappropriate behavior using the following questions as a basis for discussion:

- *How is the behavior a problem for you?* Explore how a problem impacts the teacher's interactions and efficacy at school. For example, a teacher might admit that anger and hostility often result in headaches or a feeling of guilt about how colleagues have been treated. If teachers are unable to recognize that their behavior causes serious problems for them in terms of their performance or ability to work productively with colleagues, parents, students, or the principal, they are unlikely to change.
- *What are the good and the bad things about your behavior?* There are many reasons why teachers continue to do rude, dangerous, irrational, or destructive things. These behaviors

often give them a sense of control. In some instances, dysfunctional behaviors can keep colleagues at a distance and protect teachers from being hurt or disappointed. Or some teachers like the extra attention they get from the principal when they act inappropriately. Like some of their students, teachers often consider negative attention preferable to no attention. The positives that teachers derive from being dysfunctional are often not as obvious to you as the negatives, but they need to be explored if teachers are serious about change.

- *Are you really interested in changing your behavior?* Don't assume that teachers are willing to change unless you pose this question and they respond in the affirmative. Note that you are not exploring the underlying reasons for their behavior. That is the purview of professionals. Remain focused on helping the teacher to eliminate the behavior in a firm but caring and supportive way.

- *If you are willing to make a change, what do you think you can do? What are you willing to try? What do you think the first step is? How do you think I can help you?* The key to success is isolating one behavior. Before you adjourn the meeting, summarize what you and the teacher have agreed on and who will do what and when.

Practice using the following communication techniques during Stage 3:

Ask simple, open-ended questions. When you request a response from teachers in Step 7 of your AI presentation, you are in reality asking an open-ended question. If you have a difficult time remembering the difference between closed and open questions, think about a dinner table discussion you may have had at one time with your school-aged child about what happened during the day. If you asked, "What did you learn in school today?" the answer is likely to be, "Nothing." You have asked a closed question. To open up the conversation, try phrasing your inquiry this way: "Tell me about school today." This question cannot be answered with a one-word response, thus forcing your child to reflect for a moment before answering. That is the atmosphere you want to create in Stage 3.

Listen reflectively. Listening is more than just remaining silent, although in Stage 2, remaining silent is crucial. During Stage 3, however, think critically about the meaning and intent of what the teacher is saying so that you can make productive responses. One knee-jerk reaction from you can turn a teacher off and destroy the motivational aspect of the process. Thomas Gordon (1970) suggests avoiding the following kinds of responses that do not constitute reflective listening:

- Ordering, directing, or commanding
- Warning, cautioning, or threatening
- Giving advice, making suggestions, or providing solutions
- Persuading with logic, arguing, or lecturing
- Telling people what they should do, moralizing
- Disagreeing, judging, criticizing, or blaming
- Agreeing, approving, or praising
- Shaming, ridiculing, or labeling
- Interpreting or analyzing
- Reassuring, sympathizing, or consoling
- Probing, interrogating
- Withdrawing, distracting, humoring, or changing the subject

Judiciously affirm. In this context, affirming means to cautiously give encouragement to teachers in recognition of the steps they are taking to change inappropriate behaviors.

Summarize. If you sense that teachers have reached conclusions or made specific decisions regarding what they intend to do, briefly summarize to reinforce what has been said.

Lead teachers to recognize and advocate for change in their lives. The goal of the Stage 3 motivational interview is to lead teachers to make their own case for change and then defend their arguments to you. If *you* try to convince teachers of the benefits of change or direct them to change to suit your purposes, they will automatically take the defensive position and talk themselves out of changing. For example, a statement such as, "You seem to be very comfortable with your behavior," could actually motivate the teacher to tell you that you're very wrong that the behavior is disliked or even hated, and it would be great to change it. Hearing these words from one's own mouth reinforces positive feelings regarding change. Conversely, if you criticize or analyze the behavior, the teacher is quite likely to respond defensively. "I suppose you're the perfect principal telling me what to do. *I'll* decide when to change" (adapted from Miller & Rollnick, 2002, pp. 65–81, Rollnick et al., 1999, p. 30).

Q & A

Joe: How do you set the stage for AIs?

Elaine: You don't need a stage or even any props to conduct AIs. Decide to acknowledge the elephant, schedule a meeting, and do it. The only prerequisite for AIs is that you, the individual playing the lead in this drama, have learned your lines and rehearsed the "scene" until you can "act" in a calm, respectful, and supportive manner.

HOW TO CONDUCT ASSERTIVE INTERVENTIONS

Reflect

Before you conduct AIs, reflect on your personal values, the mission of your school, what's going well, and what's not working. Think about how the teacher you intend to confront is interfering with the school's mission or undermining its positive culture. Use data rather than personal feelings or opinions to support your statements. Don't write your presentation script until you have the big picture in mind.

Read the Negotiated Contract

AIs must be conducted within the parameters of your district's negotiated contract. Read it carefully and then consult with your human resource director or superintendent to clarify any questions. In some districts, the presence of a union representative is mandated at any meeting held by a principal to discuss teachers' job performance. In other districts, the presence of a union representative is by invitation from the individual teacher. In some districts, principals are required to state the purpose of the meeting, or the teacher is not contractually obligated to attend. These procedures vary widely from state to state and district to district, hence the importance of carefully following all contractual specifications. If you are following the ten commandments of dealing with difficult teachers found in Chapter 1, you need not be concerned about the presence of a union representative during AIs. In my experience, union representatives will often act as behind-the-scenes allies in dealing with difficult teachers, especially those whose inappropriate behaviors are harmful to children. The key to working cooperatively with union representatives during AIs is to be honest, fair, and respectful with all parties involved.

Choose the Teacher

You may have multiple candidates for AIs in your school—teachers who are angry, troubled, exhausted, or just plain confused. To avoid tackling too many problems at once, apply the educational triage model: Choose the teacher who is doing the most damage to the culture and achievement of your school. That individual may well be a "toxic teacher-leader" who is fomenting revolt and taking others off mission or it could be an individual who is potentially toxic to students. (See the case studies in Chapters 4 and 6.)

Identify the Teacher's Behavior

Once you have chosen a candidate for your first AI, identify the inappropriate behavior that you want the teacher to eliminate and explicitly define it to your satisfaction. You may need to write several drafts of the definition before it is succinct.

Write Your Presentation

Now you are ready to write your AI *presentation*. Don't worry if the teacher's behavior is long standing and you have either ignored it or been inconsistent in your approach. Explain the reasons for your delay during the presentation. Consult the examples cited earlier. Choose each word carefully. Rehearse your presentation several times with someone you trust until your delivery is smooth. For maximum effect, memorize your script and put away your notes. Make sure you are comfortable with the words you have chosen and are able to make each statement in a relaxed and confident manner.

Exhibit 2.2 is a sample AI presentation to Jane, an angry teacher. As you read this example, consider how you might phrase a similar presentation to one of your angry teachers. Remember, a presentation is a sincere and honest expression of *your feelings*

Exhibit 2.2   Assertive Intervention: Jane

Name: Jane   Date: October 7

Prompt	Principal's Statement
Behavior to be eliminated	Jane, I want to talk with you about the effect that your hostility is having on the climate of our faculty meetings.
Explicit description of the behavior	Yesterday, you alternately rolled your eyes, smirked, and shook your head back and forth during the leadership team's presentation of the school improvement plan. You also made pejorative remarks in an undertone about our lowest-performing students, calling the at-risk students "welfare kids" and referring to our English language learners as "wetbacks," and then you stomped out of the meeting before it ended.

Prompt	Principal's Statement
Principal's feelings about the behavior	I'm upset by your behavior and worried about how it impacts your relationships with colleagues, the culture of our school, and your reputation as a professional.
Explanation of how the behavior impacts the teacher	I care about all of the teachers on the faculty, including you. Perhaps you weren't aware that there were members of the PTA Council and the school board at the meeting. I'm afraid that what you did during the faculty meeting is now being talked about all over town.
Principal's personal contribution to the continuance of the behavior	I should have talked to you the first time I observed your behavior at the beginning of the year, but I ignored it hoping one of your colleagues would confront you.
Principal's desire to resolve the issue	I am committed to resolving this issue. I'd like to know, when we leave my office today, that we won't ever have to discuss this problem again.
Principal's invitation to the teacher to respond	Jane, I want to understand what's going on here from your perspective. Talk to me about your feelings.

and observations. Someone else's words can only provide a model; your words communicate *your* values, beliefs, and desires.

Schedule the Meeting

Once you have written and rehearsed your presentation, make an appointment with the teacher. In some districts, you are contractually obligated to specify the reason for the meeting. If not, just say that you have something important to discuss. If you raise a teacher's level of concern, you may gain more leverage in your efforts to motivate change.

Q & A

Scott: How do you limit the negative effects of AIs on the climate of the school?

Elaine: I can tell from your question that you are worried about the consequences of conducting an AI with an especially negative teacher. Perhaps you envision the individual heading out of your office to immediately stir up trouble. So what else is new? If you're conducting an AI, the teacher's negative behavior is *already* causing trouble. Don't worry about what people might think of you. Do the right thing!

Prepare for the Meeting

As you prepare for the meeting, follow these guidelines:

- Notify the appropriate individuals of the meeting's time and place in accordance with district policies and the negotiated contract. Make sure the meeting is conducted in complete privacy with no danger of interruptions. Turn off your computer, cell phone, pager, and office phone *and* instruct your secretary not to interrupt you except for a life-threatening emergency.
- Have a box of Kleenex at hand in case the meeting turns tearful, bottled water for dry mouths, and paper on which to take notes if needed.
- Ask your secretary to remain at her desk to call for help if you suspect the teacher might become distraught or aggressive or lose control.

Conduct the AI

Greet the teacher in a pleasant way, but don't fall into a guilt trap and hand out gratuitous compliments. Keep the meeting focused on the teacher's inappropriate behavior. Never conduct an AI sitting behind your desk. Sit beside the teacher at a round table. Before you begin to speak, take several deep breaths, relax your body, and deliver your presentation as written and rehearsed. Once you have extended an invitation to the teacher to respond (Step 7 of the presentation phase), sit back and *stop talking*. The rest is up to the teacher.

You will discover that if you can stand the wait, it will be worth it. Don't become uncomfortable or impatient while you are waiting for the teacher to respond. The secret to a successful AI is to sit expectantly but calmly looking at the teacher. Don't have a staredown, but don't chatter. American comedian Josh Billings said, "Silence is one of the hardest arguments to refute." Use silence to your advantage.

Let's examine some possible ways that Stage 2 might unfold using the example from Exhibit 2.1. Jane is the angry teacher and for the purposes of this discussion, *you* are the principal who has just delivered the presentation shown in the exhibit.

Once given the invitation to respond, if Jane says, "I don't have anything to say right now," then you might say, "Well, if you *did* have something to say, what would it be?" If she refuses to answer, you might respond, "I have no idea what's going on here, Jane, but I *could* make a good guess, if you won't talk to me about how you feel."

At that point, you might venture a guess about the reasons for her behavior: "Maybe you feel left out of the process and are resentful that you weren't chosen to be a member of the School Improvement Team. So, your way of getting back at me and the teachers on the team is to poke holes in the plan they developed."

If that interpretation doesn't register with Jane, try another one: "Maybe a grade-level colleague accused you of being responsible for low achievement, and you are so upset over what she said that you're doing whatever you can to undermine the plan."

If Jane responds by saying, "You couldn't possibly understand," ask her to take a stab at explaining things. Again, wait in silence while Jane collects her thoughts. Sit quietly. Don't fidget, tap your fingers, twist your hair, or shuffle your papers.

At this point, Jane may tell you that she has been under a lot of stress lately since her husband just moved out. She may go on to say that she feels terrible about her behavior and is humiliated by her poor judgment. Bingo! Now the two of you can move on to explore how she wants to tackle the problem and how you can help her.

Or perhaps Jane will tell you that all of these "improvement initiatives" have been tried before and didn't work then, so what's the point. She might say, "The kids are lazy, and the parents don't care." Statements like these are clues that Jane is feeling unprepared for the challenges of teaching the recent influx of at-risk students in her classroom. She may be angry about what she perceives as more work, work she doesn't know how to do. This is a good time to talk about collaboration with colleagues and how much you need her expertise on your team.

Sometimes teachers' responses during Stage 2 will make *you* feel defensive. This is a natural reaction, but refrain from *saying* or *doing* anything defensive or even *looking* defensive in response. Another secret to conducting a successful AI is to differentiate yourself from Jane and realize that *you* are not the problem. *Jane's behavior* is the problem. Here are some statements that Jane might make and possible ways that you can refocus the discussion on how her behavior is impacting the morale of the school community or the level of student achievement.

Jane:	My personal life is none of your business.
Principal:	If your personal life is affecting your performance as a professional, it is my concern. Your inappropriate behavior is unprofessional.
Jane:	This doesn't involve you at all.
Principal:	If your personal life impacts the way you treat students, colleagues, or parents, it does involve me. The school community is my responsibility, and if your behavior interferes with our goals, it concerns me.
Jane:	You just don't like me.

Principal: I do like you, but I cannot accept the way you are currently behaving. It is because I like you that I want to help you deal with the issues that are keeping you from being the professional educator I know you can be.

Jane: You have no right to talk to me like that.

Principal: My job description requires that I supervise and evaluate every teacher in this building. I'm expected by law to protect the safety and well-being of every aspect of this school, and your behavior falls under that umbrella. I have the responsibility to make sure that we leave no child behind, and one part of that responsibility is making sure that all teachers are doing their share.

It may be that Jane will totally clam up and refuse to talk. That means she is not ready to face reality yet. She still believes that she can behave inappropriately and get away with it. However, her refusal to talk about the issue doesn't mean that you will stop pointing it out to her in explicit and direct terms. Don't let Jane's inability to face up to her behavior take you off course. Glance at your watch and set up another meeting for the following week. When Jane asks what the meeting will be about, tell her, "You know what the meeting will be about, Jane."

Keep confronting Jane with reality. Follow author Anne Lamott's (1994) advice in this kind of situation: "You don't always have to chop with the sword of truth. You can point with it, too" (p. 156). Ask more questions. Keep asking open-ended questions to determine how Jane feels about this problem. Beware of talking too much, and never take ownership of her problem or empathize in a heartfelt moment of pity. It's Jane's problem, not yours!

Don't end your meeting prematurely, panicked at what may seem to be your lack of success. Be ready for some long silences. Let Jane be the one who panics and starts to babble. Don't allow anything or anyone to interrupt this meeting; you will lose the momentum and emotional impact you have gained. Don't assume that you have made any progress toward eliminating the problem until Jane acts appropriately for the first time at a faculty meeting. However, when she does make a move in that direction, notice it and commend her privately. But don't think Jane has had a temperament transplant. There will be setbacks. If you care about Jane's contribution to the goals of your school community, keep pointing the way to her.

If Jane's inappropriate behavior persists even after she has indicated a willingness to work on it, conduct another AI. She may be testing your resolve in dealing with her behavior, or she may need professional help. Undoubtedly she has had prior experiences with administrators who mentioned her problem once and when that didn't work, ignored her thereafter. Or perhaps you haven't been persistent in dealing with her behavior up to this point and need to convince her that *you* have changed. It could be that if someone on the leadership team also conducts an AI with Jane (see case study in Chapter 3), she will more readily face up to the feelings that are driving her behavior, whether insecurity regarding her ability to deliver instruction, gut-wrenching family problems, anger at the unfairness of how the team members were chosen, or a feeling of powerlessness that often overcomes teachers when they find themselves out of control.

Deal with Jane or any tough teacher by setting high expectations. Communicate that you believe she is capable of eliminating her inappropriate behavior and that you are committed to helping her achieve this goal. If possible, before the meeting ends, agree on what will happen next and how you will help to hold her responsible. However, if you do run out of time, schedule another meeting when both you and Jane have had time to reflect and can then complete Stage 3 more productively. Be sure to summarize orally what has happened at the meeting and then follow up with a written summary. In both the oral and written summaries, include what is planned for the follow-up meeting, and what, if anything, you and Jane (or your difficult teacher) will do in the interim.

Q & A

Tom: What if a teacher doesn't eliminate an inappropriate behavior after I've conducted my first AI?

Elaine: Conducting an AI is no guarantee that a teacher will miraculously morph into a Golden Apple Award Winner, particularly if the problem is a persistent one. But if you have the courage to conduct the first AI with a teacher, your odds of eventually succeeding (i.e., the teacher changes, resigns, or is dismissed) increase exponentially. If you never start, your school culture will slowly crumble from within. Conducting an AI can't make things worse. The climate might get temporarily chilly, but the weather *will* improve dramatically if you persevere. An AI can also be the first step in gathering the evidence needed to dismiss a teacher.

Deal With the Fallout

Be prepared for the emotional reactions you may experience after you deal with difficult teachers. Cathie West describes her feelings this way:

When it comes to dysfunctional teachers, I go through the stages of grief. First, I deny that I need to take serious action. Then I am angry that a teacher I've spent untold hours helping is still incompetent, and finally, I get depressed over what I know will follow. So I prepare myself for a huge emotional hit. I don't enjoy the resentment that will come from the teacher, the antagonism that will pour forth from the union, or the anxiety that will pervade my faculty while this work is being done. I am always at my lowest after delivering bad news to teachers at formal conferences with union representatives. I dislike seeing teachers in distress when they are reprimanded, and I really hate getting beat up by the union while I am doing this painful job. When a meeting like this is finally over, I sometimes shut my door and weep.

So why do I do it? It's always for the children—we have to rescue them from chaotic classrooms, demeaning teachers, and the physical abuse that still goes on behind closed doors in many classrooms today. The responsibility to *do* something is painful and upsetting, but we have no choice but to be "John Wayne" and step forward with courage!

SUMMING UP

Here are the "big ideas" of Chapter 2:

- Deal one-on-one with difficult teachers, assertively, explicitly, systematically, and supportively until they: (1) face the reality of their behavior and its impact on the mission of the school, (2) feel uncomfortable and displeased with their behavior, and (3) can monitor and change their behavior on their own.
- Set high expectations for teacher conduct generally and continue to revisit the behaviors of problem teachers as often as needed.
- Maintain a positive, assertive, and relentless attitude toward any behaviors that undermine the mission of your school.

Strategies for Dealing With Angry, Hostile, or Just Plain Tiresome Teachers

Before embarking on this chapter . . .

Consider this vivid metaphor:

One angry teacher can precipitate a blaze of discontentment that runs through the school touching off other fires. The principal needs to be a good fire fighter—quickly containing problems and putting the fires out.

—Cathie West

Angry teachers remind me of porcupines. Their critical outbursts sting when they hit their targets, they are difficult to remove once placed where they have been aimed, and they often leave permanent scars—just like the quills of porcupines. But I've recently learned some new information about porcupines that might apply to angry teachers. Although porcupines are generally solitary creatures, during late fall and early winter they temporarily relax their quills in order to mate. It appears that these prickly creatures do have a soft side after all. There is also hope for prickly teachers, but only if you are prepared to conduct AIs that tell the truth explicitly and then offer angry teachers positive alternatives—opportunities for collaboration, teamwork, attention, acceptance, and affirmation.

UNDERSTANDING ANGRY TEACHERS

You no doubt have at least one teacher in mind who personifies anger for you. But consider the following definition as a more productive one to help you understand and deal with angry teachers. "Anger is an experience that occurs when a goal, value, or expectation that [teachers] have chosen has been blocked or when [their] sense of personal worth is threatened" (Taylor & Wilson, 1997, p. 71). Lots of perfectly normal teachers end up angry when they are threatened or thwarted. *Anger is a plea from unhappy individuals for attention, acceptance, and affirmation.*

Here's an example of how one angry teacher was rehabilitated when transplanted to a new culture. She was involuntarily transferred to my building after planning a mini-revolt against her principal. From the first moment I stepped into her classroom, I knew she was a highly effective teacher. I asked if she was willing to coach a new teacher who was having difficulties with classroom management. Thereafter, she was one of the most dedicated and supportive teachers in the building.

I didn't have to engage in AIs with this teacher. Placed in a positive culture, she chose to focus her talents on productive endeavors. I suspect that if we *had* discussed the reasons for her earlier difficulties, she would have identified resentment and disappointment. She resented the leadership vacuum in her former school and stepped in to take over. She was disappointed at the lack of an organized school mission and exasperated at how much time was being wasted reinventing the wheel.

Anger is a complex emotion that can signal displeasure, hurt, shame, pain, indignation, resentment, exasperation, or annoyance, all of which may range from mild to extreme. It can manifest itself in aggressive behaviors like criticizing, yelling, teasing, ridiculing, or scolding; in physical responses, such as hitting or hurting others; or in more passive ways, like silence, withdrawal, or hostile body language (Taylor & Wilson, 1997, pp. 53–54).

Later in the chapter we look at some specific ways that teachers manifest their anger, but for the moment, let's examine what works and what doesn't when dealing with angry teachers.

WHAT WORKS AND WHAT DOESN'T?

The hardest part of dealing with angry teachers is making the decision to stop ignoring them. At that point, many principals find it difficult to know exactly what to do. Here's how one principal expressed his frustration: "I've tried to be a good listener, accommodating, and understanding, but that just enables the behaviors. I've tried to be more forceful, and that results in cries of authoritarianism and accusations of unwillingness to listen to staff ideas."

Let's consider where this principal might have gone wrong. He gets high marks for figuring out that listening and empathizing don't work with angry teachers. But why didn't his "forceful" approach work? Perhaps in an effort to appear firm and in control of his teachers, he was perceived as intimidating. Rather than confronting one angry teacher at a time, he may have announced to the entire faculty that he wasn't going to tolerate certain behaviors, thereby leaving the impression that he was also angry.

Another principal is troubled by her inability to get angry teachers to recognize the damage their behavior does. Here's how she describes the situation in her school: "These teachers tend to pose problems like irritating parents by refusing to respond appropriately to them, dominating meetings with their negative comments, being moody around students and adults in the school, letting their tempers get the best of them, and blowing up at staff or parents."

Here's how she has dealt with the problems up to now. "I hold end-of-the-year conferences with all of my teachers in which we focus on areas of improvement for the next year. With angry teachers, I always put one of their problem behaviors on the table for discussion. Either I get a nod of the head indicating a willingness to work on it next year, or I get denial and blaming. Either way, nothing changes. I feel that I have confronted them regarding their anger issues, but the possibility exists that I have not been as direct as I thought or as effective as I hoped."

Let's examine how this principal might tweak her approach to get the results she desires. She could be sending mixed messages to her angry teachers. She routinely makes only one attempt each year to confront them about their anger. They have figured out that she's not really serious about it and that if they can make it through one short meeting, they'll be off the hot seat for another year.

However, there are unmistakable signs that these folks are chipping away at the positive culture of this school. According to the principal, these angry teachers "are besieged with complaints from parents and staff; are only comfortable when working with a small, select group of friends; and shun large group 'happy' activities." According to the principal, they are "capable" but not "great" teachers. Their anger is interfering not only with their personal development as teachers but also with the mission of the school.

> You cannot change others. More people suffer from trying to change others than from any other sickness. And it is impossible. What you can do is influence them.
>
> **—Cloud and Townsend (1992, p. 89)**

Exactly how *does* one deal effectively with angry teachers? First of all, "dealing" does not mean issuing ultimatums. Unless angry teachers recognize the benefits of changing their ways and conclude on their own that they need to change (see the case study later in this chapter), *you* cannot eliminate their inappropriate behavior and attitudes. Dealing effectively with angry teachers means responding to them in different ways than principals before you have responded. Endeavor not to control them but to point out the ways in which they can become productive and satisfied staff members. To deal effectively with angry teachers, conduct as many AIs as are necessary to communicate this message: "Either become a positive and productive teacher-leader *or* a collaborative and supportive team player, *or* get out of the way. You are taking too much of my time and energy that could be devoted to achieving the mission of our school."

Most angry teachers have never been confronted in this way. Furthermore, most of them are used to having their problems ignored, underestimated, or even demeaned as some sort of a bad joke, which often makes them even angrier. They don't want to be ignored. Angry teachers crave acknowledgement, attention, acceptance, and affirmation. In their opinion, their problems are never given the kind of recognition they deserve.

Principals' Roundtable: What Works and What Doesn't?

Elaine: Let's begin by talking about what *hasn't* worked for you in dealing with angry teachers.

Doug Pierson: I've found that angry teachers are usually those with the most teaching experience. The profession has changed a great deal since they began teaching, and they haven't changed with it. These angry teachers would like it to be the way it was in the "good old days."

Elaine: So what methods have you tried to solve this pervasive problem?

Carol Kottwitz: I've tried sending memos to teachers outlining their unacceptable behaviors and setting forth the desired behaviors that are necessary. This strategy sometimes works, but other times, teachers will pull in the union. Then my hands get slapped.

Elaine: What about just ignoring inappropriate behavior?

Kathy Johnson: Ignoring a problem doesn't work. That sends a signal to other staff members that I either approve of the behavior or am "afraid" to confront it.

Kathie Dobberteen: But just talking to these teachers in a sensible way doesn't seem to make much impact either.

Jim Ratledge: Early on, I would sometimes be slow to get involved (unless students were affected), hoping that the situation would improve. That rarely happened.

Mark Frankel: I've tried to get teachers like this involved with a team, but getting other people to collaborate with them when they are choosing to isolate themselves is a real challenge.

Elaine: You've certainly tried a variety of approaches that *haven't* been successful. Let's hear about what *does* work for you.

Kathie Dobberteen: I point out concrete examples of their behavior, both effective and ineffective, similar to AIs. When I'm working with a more difficult teacher, I use the FRISK (Andelson, 2001) model for documenting behavior and needed corrective actions. (See Chapter 6 for more information about FRISK.)

Mark Frankel: If I'm lucky, I'm able to identify a person's idiosyncratic needs, whether for recognition, approval, security, or power. Then I have the key to helping people feel that I recognize and value their needs sincerely. People have to see the need for change in terms of their homeostasis (i.e., being unhappy or uncomfortable enough so that changing their behavior will improve their present situation).

Jim Ratledge: Our system is blessed with a number of mental health support services that are available to all staff in a confidential, caring environment. Apprising teachers of these services and encouraging their participation in a supportive, nonthreatening manner has been very successful.

Craig Spiers: We also have a confidential Employee Assistance Program that I can offer to staff in need. I can work on eliminating the inappropriate behaviors at school and be assured that a professional is helping teachers with the issues in their lives that have precipitated their behaviors.

Shirley Johnson: My fallback for dealing with angry teachers is what I call a "Come to Jesus" meeting.

Elaine: Can you explain what that is?

Shirley Johnson: I call a meeting with a teacher to outline what I deem to be unacceptable about their work performance. At that time, they may ask for "forgiveness."

Elaine: Sounds like a "spiritual" version of an AI. What if they don't ask for forgiveness or are totally unconcerned about their behavior?

Shirley Johnson: Well, I do have a number of variations on this theme, depending on the teacher and the problem. Sometimes I restrict their options for extra assignments, and this takes money out of their pockets. That works.

Elaine: What else has worked for the rest of you?

Lydia Zuidema: Of course hiring good teachers in the first place reduces the number of problems, but consistency, speaking the truth in love, accountability, and documentation have all worked for me.

Carol Kottwitz: The best way that I've found to assist teachers in this category is to conference with them. The meetings don't always go smoothly, so I schedule them on Friday afternoons. I have found that given enough time, teachers will usually reflect on their performance, and we can work out specific strategies that guarantee success. Sometimes it takes time for teachers to face the reality of their behavior. When teachers apply for a transfer and no one wants them, they may suddenly decide it's in their best interests to change.

Doug Pierson: I have also found that taking the direct approach is the most successful. I believe most folks would rather hear about concerns or issues directly and to the point. This should be done in private with just the principal and teacher present, unless there may be any kind of disciplinary repercussions. Then, a supportive union representative should be invited by the teacher.

Kathy Johnson: It's important to be bold and take a stand so that other faculty members know you can handle problems. They need to feel that their leader has things under control.

Ron Collins: Some angry teachers have no business being in the classroom with children. They need confrontation, evaluation, documentation, and ultimately, dismissal. Of course while all this is going on, students are forced to endure substandard teachers.

Elaine: But if not now, when? And if not you, then who?

KINDS OF ANGRY TEACHERS

Angry teachers come in a variety of colors, styles, and sizes, but they fall into two basic groups: angry teachers who *can* teach and those who *can't*. When angry teachers are instructionally effective, your prospects for helping them to eliminate unproductive behaviors are excellent. (See the case study later in this chapter.) If your angry staff members *can't* teach, you will have to decide which problem to confront first. See Chapter 6 for ways to deal with marginal and incompetent teachers.

Once you have identified the angry teachers who *can* teach, divide that group into three categories: (1) aggressive, (2) passive-aggressive (sneaky), and (3) passive-aggressive (tiresome). Knowing the ways that teachers display and use their anger to achieve what they want may provide insights regarding the reasons behind it.

Aggressive Teachers

Aggressive expressions of anger, whether physical or verbal, are easy to identify. They are up-front and in your face. Aggressive teachers *intend* to be hurtful, obstructive, and demeaning. They are dangerous, hostile, have no qualms about launching their attacks in public, and sometimes even become physical when threatened. Aggressive teachers can terrorize colleagues, students, and parents, not to mention the principal. If left unconfronted, they can destroy a positive school culture. Eavesdrop on what four aggressive teachers have to say about how they feel. You may recognize someone you know.

Naysayers

"I just can't believe the crazy ideas these people come up with: Planning for Improvement, Achievement for the 21st Century, and No Child Left Behind. Administrators are just too much. We should leave a few of them behind the next time the school board puts the budget together. Well, just wait until the faculty meeting. I have a mile-long list of reasons why the improvement plan the team dreamed up won't work."

Cynics

"I spoke my piece at the faculty meeting tonight. I didn't exactly get a standing ovation, but I told it like it is. If they think some wimpy legislation is going to change the way I do business, they've got another think coming. They've tried this stuff before. Head Start, The Great Society, Title I, Special Ed. They just keep giving different names to the same old stuff. Include everybody. Teach everybody. All can learn. Right!"

Perfectionists (Complainers)

"My goal in life is to do things right. Unfortunately, my colleagues are more interested in getting it done than in getting it done right. And the principal is no better. She's slapdash about spelling, and the punctuation in the faculty bulletin needs remediation. On top of that she has absolutely no taste. And then there are all these young teachers. They spend more time on their makeup than on lesson plans. No wonder our scores are low."

> There's an important distinction between respecting a person in the sense that we admire and hold that person in especially high esteem and treating that person with respect. While respecting others is desirable, respectfulness is morally mandatory. Thus, people of character treat everyone with respect, even those who are not personally respectworthy.
>
> —*Michael Josephson (2004)*

Bombasters

"I'm sick and tired of all the things we start around here and never finish. We've got about fifty goals this year, and if we accomplish one of them, it'll be a miracle. I'm going in to see the principal after school and give him a piece of my mind. I did use a few four-letter words the last time I met with him. But nothing else seems to get his attention."

Passive-Aggressive Teachers

While aggressive teachers are impossible to ignore, passive-aggressive teachers disguise their intense anger in subtle and hard-to-confirm ways. At first glance, they may seem to be irresponsible individuals or people with personality problems. In reality, they are sneaky and tiresome angry teachers.

Characteristics of Sneaky Teachers

Passive-aggressive (sneaky) teachers deny they are angry; say one thing and do another; walk away; and refuse to cooperate, compromise, or concede. They love to manipulate you by sliding out from under the immediate consequences that usually come down on aggressive teachers. There are also the more dangerous types of passive-aggressive teachers, like backstabbers and saboteurs—the individuals who have packaged their anger in such a way as to undermine and overthrow your authority.

Q & A

Beth: Do you have any suggestions for dealing with a teacher who always hands things in late but who always has an excuse or reason?

Elaine: You have a classic case of passive-aggressive anger. There's only one way to deal with this individual. Conduct an AI. Bring her face to face with the reality of her behavior and the message it is sending to the rest of the faculty, her students (who eventually learn about juicy gossip like this through the grapevine), and to the office staff who have to put up with her nonsense. This individual sets a bad example for everyone. For that reason she is impeding the achievement of your mission.

My opening statement to this persistent procrastinator would go something like this: "Sharon, I asked to meet with you today because I'm very distressed about your inappropriate behavior, namely your total disregard for deadlines. Your behavior sets a very bad example for your students, and it's undermining the positive culture we've established at our school. I'm sorry that I haven't brought this up to you sooner. I shouldn't have waited so long."

Sharon will be shocked. She thought she had you fooled, and now she knows that you know that she's not just careless and flaky. She's mad! Don't take it personally. It's not about you. Put your own emotions into neutral and be a healthy role model for this teacher. The best way to point this sneaky teacher in a more positive direction is with recognition for her strengths and talents, plus lots of encouragement and support.

It's sometimes difficult to determine whether a teacher's failure to turn in lesson plans, come to school on time, or pay attention during faculty meetings are passive-aggressive expressions of anger or just coincidental cases of bad manners and poor time management. The more subtle the passive-aggressive behaviors, the more difficult it can be to pin down the perpetrators. But if you pay close attention, you can usually sense their hostility simmering just beneath the surface.

In some instances, passive-aggressive teachers may not even realize that their "minor misbehaviors" are the result of hostility. They often see themselves as free spirits and consider their attitudes of noncompliance to be expressions of individuality and independence. The critical attribute of sneaky passive-aggressive anger is its *intent*. If a teacher refuses to speak to you in the hallway because her hearing aid battery went dead, that's one kind of behavior. If she ignores you with intent to snub you and then denies it, that's passive-aggressive anger.

Q & A

Gary: How do you deal with teachers who exhibit all of the characteristics that they don't accept in their students (late reports, rude responses, and tardiness) but feel that they are excellent teachers?

Elaine: Teachers like these are both angry and misguided. They believe that being an excellent teacher is unrelated to being a person of character. When teachers openly defy rules that their colleagues must follow, they are subtly undermining the culture of your school and blatantly interfering with the attainment of its mission. They are communicating an attitude of disrespect for you that is unacceptable, showing their colleagues that they don't have to follow the rules, and saying to their students, "Do what I say, not what I do." The only way to deal with teachers like these is to conduct AIs in which you name their behavior for what it is—anger, disrespect, dishonesty, or insubordination.

One or more of the following behaviors, when consistently evident in teachers, are symptoms of passive-aggressive anger: reading the newspaper or knitting during a faculty meeting or inservice session; joking and kidding (often in semisarcastic and hurtful ways); acting confused; being habitually late, being easily distracted (acting as though everything is more important than what another person is saying); exaggerating the principal's bad habits; putting oneself down in an effort to solicit pity; agreeing with everything using passive comments, such as "Sure, do whatever you want"; being passively resistant (insisting on having one's own way no matter what); crying to seek sympathy; minimizing a colleague's accomplishments; feigning deafness; arguing; laughing off a colleague's comments; pouting to seek sympathy; constantly questioning, arguing, and being oppositional; stating that one is not angry and denying any subversive intentions; sending double messages (saying one thing and doing another); procrastinating; doing things far better than they need to be done to make others feel inadequate or guilty; constantly making silly mistakes; being inefficient and thus unable to complete certain tasks; undereating or overeating; getting sick all the time (seeking sympathy, willing oneself ill out of feelings of hurt, bitterness, helplessness, or frustration); being clumsy (e.g., breaking things on purpose); walking away from a situation and passively withdrawing; gossiping and spreading malicious rumors about other colleagues or the principal; overinvolvement (overextending oneself as a way of avoiding more important responsibilities); and lying (Hankins & Hankins, 1988, pp. 30-32).

Perhaps you are dealing with one or more of the following underappreciated and underaffirmed sneaky teachers. If so, these monologues may sound familiar.

Backstabbers/Saboteurs

"I've given the best years of my life to this school, and nobody ever writes me up in the weekly bulletin. I guess you've got to be young and cute to catch the new principal's eye. It doesn't matter how much you know, and I know plenty, believe me. But it only counts if you're doing some new-fangled thing brought in by some overpriced consultant. Drive-by staff development. I wonder what I'd have to do to get noticed. Maybe I'll file a grievance."

> The most difficult type of teacher with whom I have worked is one who undermines authority and works to sabotage not only what I do but also what other teachers do. This kind of person can be slippery and difficult to catch in the act, and it drains the principal's time and energy as well as causing insomnia.
>
> —*Principal Sue Braithwaite*

Gossips

"I saw the principal having lunch with that new central office administrator last week. They were huddled in a booth looking very cozy. It looked like they were talking about more than test scores. You know, if she would do something with her hair, she could be attractive. I understand from a friend of mine who worked in a school where she used to be the principal that she's quite the carouser. Now, please don't tell anyone where you heard this."

Liars

"Of course I called Mrs. Smith back when you asked me to. What reason would I have for lying about it? It's no wonder that woman's kids are so irresponsible the way she can't tell the truth from a lie. After all, who are you going to believe, a single mother or someone who's been teaching for twenty-five years?"

Characteristics of Tiresome Teachers

Teachers in the second passive-aggressive category are "tiresome." The tiresome types are easy to spot. They are either (1) talking nonstop, (2) interrupting constantly, (3) pontificating pompously, (4) telling the same bad jokes over and over, or (5) making humorous sarcastic remarks at the expense of others. Some tiresome types are able to manage all five behaviors at the same time. Although these teachers may appear to be socially inept, most are frustrated and angry at being ignored and isolated by their colleagues. If you are tempted to excuse these often overbearing individuals who apparently don't know any better, think again. Any behavior that interferes with your school mission or sabotages a positive school culture is worthy of attention. Here are three tiresome teachers doing what they are always doing: talking.

Know-It-Alls

"You want to know about effective instruction. Let *me* fill you in. I just attended a workshop, and it was fantastic. Actually, I already knew everything they covered. It was all of that Madeline Hunter stuff from years ago. I attended several of her workshops in the 80s. She was a wonderful person. Actually, I knew her personally."

Jokesters

"You need a good story for the faculty meeting? Well, have you heard this one? A mother goes in to wake up her son to go to school. He groans and rolls over to face the wall. `I don't want to go to school today,' he whines. `The kids don't like me and neither do the teachers.' His mother shakes his shoulder and says, "You have to go to school. You're the principal.' Isn't that a good one? I've got another great one you might like . . . "

Compulsive Talkers

"I have no idea about what I'm going to do today for my fourth-period class. It's a great group of kids, but they're so scattered and disorganized. We're working on the Civil War, but I'm just not crazy about that period of history. What do you think I should do? Maybe I should just assign the chapter and then give them a quiz, but maybe that's not such a good idea. What do you think? Maybe there's a good video we could watch. I could do my nails at the same time. I love teaching. It's so flexible. So what do you think I should do?"

HOW TO DEAL WITH ANGRY TEACHERS

The most effective way to deal with angry teachers is to conduct AIs. Chapter 2 described the critical attributes of AIs and provided a sample script of a principal's presentation to Jane, a hostile and highly critical teacher (Exhibit 2.2). Here are some specific guidelines for conducting AIs with angry teachers.

- Angry teachers may well request the presence of their union representatives at their meetings with you. In some districts the presence of the union representative is a given from the very beginning. Welcome the union's involvement. It will provide a perfect opportunity for others to see your respectful approach to problem solving as well as to hear the truth about the damage being done by the angry teacher in question. If you deal positively and proactively with union representatives, they can be very helpful. As they observe the behaviors and attitudes of angry teachers escalate out of control while you continue to be reasonable and supportive, they may well work behind the scenes to ameliorate the situation.

- Accept the reality that angry teachers are *not* better left ignored or unconfronted. They undermine and deter the accomplishment of your school's mission. They diminish your leadership capabilities. They send messages to effective staff members that you condone their angry behavior. They systematically weaken or destroy a positive school culture.
- Emotionally disengage yourself from the behaviors and attitudes of angry teachers. Do not succumb to feelings of guilt, sympathy, responsibility, or anger in response.
- Remain assertive, calm, emotionally neutral, nondefensive, nonjudgmental, and respectful during all of your interactions with angry teachers. Review the Ten Commandments shown in Figure 1.1.
- Don't be manipulated into giving in to outrageous demands.
- Whenever possible, affirm the value and capitalize on the strengths of angry teachers, taking care to distinguish your feelings regarding their behavior from your feelings regarding them personally.
- If angry teachers respond actively and appropriately (i.e., they are willing to talk about their feelings and possible solutions to the problem) after you have delivered your opening sixty-second presentation, be prepared to attend and listen. Don't be impatient. Don't talk, interrupt, or rush to fill the silences that may occur. Review the A–Z Communicator's Handbook in Resource A for helpful tips.
- As long as angry teachers are willing to work on reducing and ultimately eliminating their hostility (with your support), it's not generally necessary to identify the source of their hostility. The only exception might be if some individual or situation at school continues to inflame the teacher, and a facilitator is needed to work out the disagreement.
- If angry teachers become "tiresome" and start changing the subject, interrupt them with a statement such as, "That idea might be interesting to explore at another time, but let's get back to the question we have on the table. What's your feeling about the specific behavior I've just described?" or "What's your plan for eliminating your inappropriate actions and attitudes?"

- If angry teachers respond inappropriately by making accusatory statements or becoming aggressive, interrupt them. State that since the meeting is going nowhere, you'd like to schedule another meeting for a later date. If the angry person asks "Why?" simply answer, "I think you know why." Resist the temptation to make some positive or pleasant comment at the end of the meeting. Be calm and polite, but don't give an angry teacher any reason to think that you are dropping the issue. If angry teachers deny that they are angry or that their behaviors and attitudes are inappropriate, they are simply not yet ready to face reality. The denials of an angry teacher do not change reality; there is just more work ahead for both of you. Schedule another AI.

- If angry teachers refuse to respond to you after you have made your sixty-second presentation, then hypothesize some reasonable scenarios based on what you know about the teacher (see the sample AI discussion in Chapter 2). If teachers still won't respond, then end the meeting. But don't let them off the hook. You might say, "Jim, it looks like we're not getting anywhere today, but this issue is very important to me. When can we get together again to talk about this?" Then, before Jim leaves your office, schedule another appointment.

- Be consistent and persistent in your follow-through. If you "drop the ball" even once (e.g., come late, miss, or cancel a meeting), angry teachers will use your "mistakes" as leverage, and you will lose the momentum you have gained thus far.

- Conduct as many AIs as you feel are needed. If the inappropriate behaviors and attitudes decrease, affirm the teacher's progress, but keep up the pressure until you get a productive *response* from the teacher during Phase 2 of an AI.

- If angry teachers refuse to respond productively when confronted with their inappropriate behaviors, even after several AIs, it's time to move from oral reprimands to the next step in your district's progressive discipline plan. Your goal is to help teachers confront their own inappropriate behaviors, but during that process you must also be prepared to *prove* with documentation that you adhered to the letter and spirit of the contract. A typical hierarchy of progressive discipline generally contains these steps: (1) oral warning, (2) oral reprimand, (3) misconduct meeting, (4) letter of reprimand, (5) suspension without pay, (6) recommendation for termination (Lawrence & Vachon, 2003, p. 8).

- If you decide to put your spoken AI statement in writing (either as a letter of reprimand or an interim formal evaluation), consider including the following sections: (1) your assumptions regarding why the teacher may have remained unresponsive (e.g., didn't care, disagreed, actually wanted to have a letter of reprimand in the personnel file); (2) your expectations regarding the inappropriate behaviors and attitudes (they will stop); and (3) what you must and will do (continue to monitor the behavior and hold assertive interventions that include members of the central office staff) because they are interfering with the school mission.

There are no givens when it comes to working with angry teachers. Once you make your sixty-second presentation and ask for a response, anything can happen. But you can't go wrong if you stick with these three "big ideas":

1. Angry teachers really have only three choices when it comes to being a part of achieving your school's mission— to become a part of the leadership team, to follow the lead of the leadership team, or to get out of the way (resign, request a transfer, be transferred involuntarily, or be dismissed).

2. The best choice for teachers is to acknowledge the reality of their inappropriate actions and become contributing members of the school community.

3. This choice will bring them self-respect as well as affirmation and acceptance from you and their colleagues.

A CASE STUDY: THE CRITICAL AND MEAN-SPIRITED TEACHER

You are now familiar with the various types of angry teachers, perhaps have written your first script, and are ready to conduct an AI. However, before you schedule an appointment with *your* angry teacher, take a few moments to see how an experienced administrator dealt with one angry teacher in her school. The author of the following case study is an experienced principal in a western state (nearly ten years in two schools) who had been dealing with an angry teacher over a three-year period. She tells the story in her own words.

Case Study: Susan

"I have one angry teacher (we'll call her Susan) who although very effective in the classroom, sabotages team building. Dealing with her hostility has taken three years of assertive interventions plus untold hours spent with other staff members to help them be more appropriate and avoid triangulation with me. Susan has recently gone through a very lengthy separation and divorce from an abusive husband. Ignoring her rudeness to others, her gossiping, and face making didn't work because it sent a signal to other staff members that I either approved of her behavior or was 'afraid' to confront the problem.

"During the first formal evaluation I had with her after I arrived in the building (at the end of my first year), I told Susan that I would be monitoring her team-building skills during the next school year. I noted that she was magnificent in nearly every way but that I didn't feel she was a team player, that she used her influence and power to often undercut and undermine the staff. She was indignant and appalled, not only by what I said but by the fact that I had written it in the evaluation. I told her that she had much to offer to others but that her instructional skills were overshadowed and diminished by her cutting attacks on others as well as by her constant gossip about her colleagues. Until

I confronted her, I don't think she realized how often she hurt others. She asked me to tell her whenever I was made aware that she had hurt someone so that she could rectify the situation. I don't think she thought I would, but I did—every time. At first it was almost weekly. Then she began to see the patterns in her behavior, was able to check herself, and in most cases, bite her tongue. She improved, but there were definitely some rough spots along the way.

"One incident involved her intimidation of two new teachers. She felt they weren't spending enough time getting to know her and her two cronies who have been here ruling the school for a very long time. She felt that the newcomers weren't following the traditional rules and procedures by paying homage in a sense to the elders in the school. In reality, she was so abrasive and threatening that the novice teachers avoided her whenever possible. They rarely went into the lounge when she was there. At that point, I began working with the rest of the staff who I trusted, and they in turn encouraged and protected the newcomers.

"It was amazing to me how the entire staff had avoided any confrontation with Susan to that point. Even when they or their friends were deeply hurt by her cutting remarks, they simply took it. Susan is eloquent but very caustic, and it's almost impossible to out-talk her. She was especially hard on anyone new and so while this incident was going on, I asked her to my office to confirm her concerns about the new teachers, the ones that she had expressed in the form of insults to the staff. I always prefaced my remarks by saying that it was important to me that I remain aware of what was wrong in the building so that I could be involved in the fixing of any problems. What she quickly learned was that the rest of the staff trusted me enough to share their reactions after her attacks on them. I had to work with both parties: the angry teacher to show her I wasn't going to be frightened (although I often left our meetings with a sickened feeling) and the staff who needed to learn how to confront her.

"I set an example for the staff by always treating Susan with respect and using very appropriate language. Then I had to create a mantra for the others that they could use to defend themselves and each other. They desperately needed to reclaim the integrity and professionalism of our staff. We had to be a team. I told them it would work more effectively if they did it without any interference from me. I was fortunate to have three teachers who jumped on this bandwagon together and started to ignore Susan's looks and body language, confront the rumors she spread by setting things straight, and maintain a united front against her by defending others when they were attacked.

"It took three years of working with the rest of the team to enable them to be strong enough to overcome their own fears and stand up to her in positive ways without being destructive. The third year was amazing. But I am not yet done with this.

"Susan is efficient and effective in the classroom but still very critical of those who aren't doing what she thinks is best. She judges others and me harshly. Her impact on the school as a whole is finally diffused because she no longer has an audience. I hired nine new staff members in three years and was able to remove one member of her triumvirate through retirement.

"Susan's anger, brought on by personal problems, probably needs to be addressed through counseling or therapy since her treatment of others seems to reflect the same type of treatment she received from her abusive husband. However, dealing with her angry behavior in a direct, timely, and consistent way has diminished its impact on the culture of our school.

"My most important job as a principal is to build relationships. I've always believed that. In three years, I have established trust and gained respect from my staff, most parents, students, and colleagues around the state. I have no special gifts, but I always start with trust. The important thing is that Susan really liked me, despite all that happened. I never embarrassed her publicly. I always lifted her up to peers, parents, and visitors. She deserved it. I don't believe her flaw is a fatal one. Everyone commented this spring on how much more united we were—how many more staff members had come forward in leadership roles and how focused we were on our vision."

SUMMING UP

The "big ideas" of Chapter 3 can be summarized as follows:

- Don't let angry, hostile, or uncooperative teachers hijack your school's mission or undermine your positive culture.

- The most productive way to deal with angry teachers who can teach is by conducting AIs.
- Be persistent, consistent, positive, trustworthy, honest, and fair in confronting angry teachers. You will see benefits for students, teachers, and parents, and also for the teachers themselves who make conscious decisions to become positive and productive faculty members.

Strategies for Dealing With Temporarily Troubled, Mentally Disordered, or Legally Compromised Teachers

Before you read this chapter . . .

Reflect on the "troubles" your faculty has seen in the past year.

Nobody knows the trouble I've seen. Nobody knows my sorrow.

—Traditional Spiritual

This chapter is about teachers who are troubled, some only temporarily as they navigate the inevitable crises of life, some so severely that they need psychological treatment or medication to function, and others to the extent that they have broken the law. One shudders at the thought of troubled individuals spending time alone with children and young people, but the reality is, they do. Dismissing troubled teachers takes time and is often as upsetting for the principal as it is for the teachers. To further complicate this issue, many troubled teachers were once or still are excellent teachers whose body chemistry, addictions, or unhealthy lifestyles make it difficult for them to maintain consistency in the classroom. They are "here" today and "gone" tomorrow. On one hand, you empathize with their difficulties, while on the other, you are deeply concerned about the academic, social, emotional, and psychological consequences of their behavior for students.

Many principals feel perfectly capable of handling angry, exhausted, and confused teachers but hide in their offices when it's time to confront a troubled one. They are afraid to do anything for fear it will be the wrong thing, and for good reason. Horror stories about dismissal proceedings for troubled teachers often involve reversal and reinstatement because the evidence was flimsy, the paperwork incomplete, or the testimony inconsistent.

John, my troubled upper-grade teacher, provides a case study regarding the challenges principals face when dealing with teachers who sexually abuse students. He was undeniably a deeply troubled man, a marginal teacher at best, who even after intensive support from a nationally known instructional coach was unable to teach a coherent lesson. Although I had no evidence, I strongly suspected John of illegal behavior outside of school. Eight years before I began working with him, he had been arrested on a charge of taking indecent liberties with a fourteen-year-old boy but was acquitted of the charges. His acquittal was viewed by his many strong supporters in the community as a vindication of his innocence. Others who were certain of his guilt blamed the local police department for botching up the trial by losing crucial evidence and bowing to political pressures.

John was very clever about the students he targeted for special attention. He never had contact with his current students outside of school. He waited until the boys were in middle school before inviting them to his home or taking them out of state to his cabin, ostensibly to hire them for odd jobs. Unfortunately, his attention was supported and encouraged by the boys' family members, often single mothers or immigrant families who were grateful for the money the boys "earned" working for John. Before she knew of John's history, one of the school board members even requested that her son be placed in John's classroom because of his reputation for nurturing and mentoring boys. Another school board member strongly believed that to automatically assign sinister motives to "caring" behaviors in the classroom was a violation of a teacher's civil rights.

When I was dealing with John, neither the superintendent nor the district's attorney suggested to me that I should call the Department of Children and Family Services to report John's behavior. At that time, sexual abuse by classroom teachers was not widely recognized or discussed. Fortunately for students everywhere, a dramatic shift in society's approach to dealing with sexual abuse and harassment has occurred in the past fifteen to twenty years. All states now have laws that require educators (principals, teachers, nurses, social workers, psychologists) to immediately report suspected physical and sexual abuse of any kind, whether by parents, guardians, or fellow educators, to district officials (as specified by school board policy) and the appropriate state agency. The language and specific requirements of the laws vary from state to state. In many states, a mandatory report to a state agency must be made *immediately* upon awareness of a problem (Arizona Department of Education, 2003). In other states (e.g., Ohio), a district compliance officer makes an initial investigation and, if the behavior constitutes child abuse, reports it to the Department of Social Services (Alleghany County Public Schools, 2004, p. 3).

In my specific situation, once John chose to stop touching students inappropriately at *school*, his behavior outside of school ceased to be relevant to me as a principal. I did not have to diagnose or treat him. I simply had to ignore the unpleasant aspects of his life and focus completely on his classroom performance. My goal had to focus on helping John become a more effective teacher.

I knew, in the light of his history, that I needed an airtight case demonstrating that I had been fair, respectful, and done everything possible to help John succeed.

Just ahead, we explore the ups and downs of dealing with troubled teachers, make a compelling case for the urgency of doing it, and illustrate how two highly effective principals (and one courageous assistant principal) dealt with troubled teachers in their schools. But first, we examine the three categories of troubled teachers: (1) temporarily troubled, (2) mentally disordered, and (3) in trouble with the law. These categories are not fixed, and the distinctions between them often blur as teachers move from one category to another. For example, temporarily troubled teachers may develop more serious problems, such as clinical depression, or react to a traumatic family problem with symptoms that when evaluated by a mental health professional suggest a personality disorder. In some instances, a problem with alcoholism that impairs teaching performance may also become a legal problem when the teacher is convicted of drunk driving.

You don't have to figure out what's wrong with your troubled teachers. Your only job is to confront their inappropriate behavior when you become aware of it, present options and opportunities for moving forward positively, support them in their efforts to change if they are willing and able, and take steps to protect the students in their classrooms if they can't.

Although you must leave the diagnosis and treatment of troubled teachers to professionals, a basic understanding of some of the more common emotional and mental traumas that can interfere with teachers' abilities to function in their classrooms is necessary.

CHARACTERISTICS OF TEACHERS WHO ARE TEMPORARILY TROUBLED

The first category of troubled teachers consists of those who are going through transitions and traumas in their lives. At any given time, every school has several staff members with family or personal problems: divorce; child custody battles; infertility;

remarriage; parenting blended families; serious or debilitating accidents; terminally ill family members; or the diagnosis of a chronic, progressive, or potentially terminal illness. Although many of the aforementioned troubles end up being anything but temporary, most mentally and emotionally healthy individuals are able to cope with the onset of problems like these; navigate through various stages of grief, acceptance, and adjustment that follow; and in most cases, resume productive and successful teaching careers.

Some teachers are intensely private and do not wish to discuss their troubles at school, either with you or their colleagues; others benefit from wordless advice (see the Communicator's A–Z Handbook for a description) and emotional support from you and their teammates. If temporarily troubled teachers are handling their difficulties, there is no reason for you to become involved. Unless there is some indication of instructional difficulties or other inappropriate behavior, be grateful that these temporarily troubled teachers are strong enough to get through tough times with their own support systems and coping mechanisms.

There are times in the life of any school, particularly a large one, in which accidents, illnesses, or deaths seem to occur almost weekly. During periods like these, teachers in a healthy school with a positive culture are able to support one another and ultimately be drawn together by their experiences. Of course, principals are not exempt from personal troubles. If you experience a traumatic event in your life, your staff members will carefully note the way you handle it. Be a character builder, as described in Chapter 1.

CHARACTERISTICS OF TEACHERS WITH MENTAL DISORDERS

I use the term *mental disorders* in this chapter cautiously. Even mental health practitioners with clinical training and experience, find diagnosing mental disorders to be challenging. However, a brief overview of this category may help you to consider a particular teacher's puzzling behavior with more insight.

Mental disorders are clinically diagnosed, based on the direct observation of individuals by mental health professionals taken in conjunction with symptoms reported by patients, rather than by any blood tests or laboratory findings. A *disorder* refers to a cluster of symptoms and signs associated with distress and impairment of functioning. The symptoms of mental disorders exist on a continuum, and the point at which abnormalities in cognition, emotion, mood, and social interaction become a clinically diagnosed disorder are open to judgment, even among mental health professionals.

Individuals with mental disorders have problems that result from chemical imbalances in their brains. Sometimes they are out of touch with reality and totally incapable of managing their classrooms, while at other times they may be brilliant teachers who make a positive impact on students. This roller-coaster behavior can leave you confused about your personal observations and perceptions. They may be suffering from depression ranging from chronic to acute, causing gloomy moods and sullen withdrawal from colleagues. Others may be self-destructive or have alcohol- or drug-related problems. Some may have bipolar disorder mood swings, and others may be diagnosed with conditions like schizophrenia or delusional disorders (Surgeon General of the United States, 1999). Mentally disordered teachers are emotionally fragile and need to be handled with sensitivity and caring. They must, however, be held accountable for their inappropriate behavior.

Although there are many categories of mental disorders enumerated and defined in the *Diagnostic and Statistical Manual of Mental Disorders* (American Psychiatric Association, 2002), only one will be described in detail here: personality disorders. There are no statistics to indicate the number of classroom teachers who suffer from clinically diagnosed personality disorders or who have what some call a borderline personality disorder (Lebelle, 2000), but you have no doubt worked with or supervised at least one individual who exhibited some or many of the following symptoms.

Teachers with personality disorders display a constellation of difficult-to-handle symptoms: unreliability, emotional instability, failure to take personal responsibility for professional responsibilities, poor judgment, and irrational anger. The most predictable thing about this category of teachers is their unpredictability. One minute they are able to convince you they've turned over a new leaf, and the next minute they are "melting down" in the front hallway. What is predictable about teachers with personality disorders is that whenever their lives outside of school are stressful, the demands of teaching intensify, their students are behaviorally challenging, or interactions with colleagues are tense, they disintegrate and revert to what psychologists call "a rigid, habitual, inappropriate, and non-constructive emotional response" (L. Lantinga & M. Schohn, personal communication, September 6, 2004).

Personality disorders cannot be considered an "illness" in the strict sense of the word, because they often do not interfere with teachers' emotional, intellectual, or perceptual functioning. They do, however, interfere with teachers having positive relationships with colleagues, students, and parents as well as being productive on the job.

Although personality-disordered teachers would like you to believe that their inadequate teaching performance is due to uncontrollable outside forces, like family, money, or health problems, the biggest problem they have is keeping their emotions under control in stress-filled situations. They are explosive and distrustful, and in many cases, they refuse to seek help even when it is available through an Employee Assistance Program (EAP), making it necessary for you to repeatedly confront them about their unprofessional and irresponsible behavior. The case studies later in the chapter illustrate ways to deal with teachers exhibiting the described behaviors.

CHARACTERISTICS OF TEACHERS WHO ARE LEGALLY COMPROMISED

Teachers in trouble with the law are those who have been accused and proven guilty of criminal behavior of three different kinds: (1) sexual misconduct, (2) abuse of controlled substances, or (3) theft and fraud. Suspected criminal misconduct, when it occurs in the school setting, must be dealt with promptly and with the involvement of your local police department. When teachers' criminal misconduct occurs outside the school setting, the procedures for dealing with it may differ, especially in cases involving tenured teachers. However, the gold standard of conduct for all teachers is their status as a role model. "When a staff member sets a bad example for students, he or she can be dismissed from the school district if sufficient evidence indicates that the person may have engaged in outside conduct that would impair on-the-job effectiveness or working relationships with staff, students, and parents" (Lawrence & Vachon, 2003, p. 81).

In the case of John, my troubled teacher, it was his conviction for sexual misconduct that ultimately removed him from the classroom. Although I had prepared a summative evaluation containing reams of documentation to support dismissal for unsatisfactory classroom performance, he was charged with five counts of aggravated criminal sexual abuse of a minor boy, pled guilty, and was sentenced before I could hold the evaluation conference.

Principals' Roundtable: Dealing With Troubled Teachers

Elaine: When I think about the troubled teachers with whom I've worked, I get an overwhelming sense of frustration and inadequacy.

Todd White: As principals, we often feel that we have to own everyone's problem and be there to "fix" things. We have to realize that others are more capable of dealing with certain situations, but we need to have those resources available to access for our staff members. The best thing is to not get into long-drawn-out discussions about the issues. Send them to get outside help, and help them to refocus on their responsibilities in the school.

Laurence Fieber: I always keep in mind the fact that I am not able to change what is not ready to be changed. I have referred faculty to professional counseling, but a person has to be ready to accept this advice. Caring and persistence are the best approaches.

Doug Pierson: I believe that at any given time, any of us can be troubled about personal issues. For the most part, I believe that these are short-term issues and go away after a period of time. I think those teachers that are truly emotionally unstable need to have their problems addressed or there is carryover to the children they serve.

Todd Lambert: You have to be a good listener and determine what you can do to keep school as stress free as possible, especially if the situation is temporary. School is stressful. No one in the education business can deny this fact. However, in the short term, I do all that I can do to make things easier for a troubled teacher. It also helps if the team dynamics are strong, and fellow teachers are understanding and capable of dealing with the problems that may arise.

Craig Spiers: I agree with what Todd has said. Although my high school has 275 staff members (both certified and classified), we consider ourselves to be a family. We care about each other, treat each other with respect, listen to each other's concerns, and come to the aid of colleagues in need. When a staff member or immediate family member is hospitalized, we send a card signed by everyone. We do the same for births and deaths. I speak personally with every staff member who has a crisis of any kind. We have a confidential EAP that I always suggest to staff in need. In order to strengthen our family, we socialize together, recognize accomplishments, and provide professional training to enhance our school's performance. My door is always open. My staff is my extended family. It's my job to support them.

Jim Ratledge: I've found that maintaining confidentiality is very important. Our system is blessed with a number of mental health support services that are available to all staff in a confidential, caring environment.

Judy Marquardt: When a teacher is experiencing life issues outside of the classroom, being empathetic while also maintaining and communicating high expectations is helpful. The teacher may well need more structure and a tighter leadership style during these time periods. People in crisis mode have to prioritize what they are focusing on, and I want to make sure that their students and the classroom learning community are among their priorities.

Cathie West: I have successfully used school counselors and staff from EAPs to help troubled teachers. I also try to be empathetic while employing William Glasser's questioning strategies: What's happening? What are *you* doing? Is this working for you? What else could you do that might work better? Are you prepared to make this change? When would you like to meet again to talk about your progress?

Todd White: Sometimes I have found that being too empathetic only reinforces the behavior of some troubled teachers. This approach allows them to be "victims" and to get out of taking responsibility for their own behavior.

Elaine: We tread a fine line as principals when we're working with troubled teachers. If you suspect that you may be part of the problem rather than the solution, it's time to back off and take a more assertive stand.

HOW TO DEAL WITH TEACHERS WHO ARE TEMPORARILY TROUBLED

The advice shared by our roundtable members regarding how they deal with troubled teachers in general is especially applicable to dealing with temporarily troubled teachers:

- Listen, and if appropriate offer wordless advice as described in the Communicator's A–Z Handbook (Resource A).
- Temporarily reduce the workload or offer assistance with release time or instructional aides.
- Be available if needed.
- Offer referral services if appropriate.
- Protect students to the greatest extent possible.
- Maintain appropriate boundaries.

HOW TO DEAL WITH TEACHERS WHO HAVE MENTAL DISORDERS

Dealing with teachers who have clinically diagnosed mental disorders or exhibit many of the inappropriate behaviors that are symptomatic of a disorder is a far more challenging assignment than listening empathetically to temporarily troubled teachers who are functioning appropriately in their classrooms. There are few careers as stressful for individuals with mental disorders as teaching.

Principals Cathie West and Cal Miller share their expertise regarding how to deal with teachers who are deeply troubled in the following case studies. These two highly capable administrators have more than four decades of experience between them and have successfully navigated the rough waters of dealing with a variety of difficult teachers. As you read their stories, look for the key principles that guided their interactions. They are summarized following the case studies.

Case Study: My Most Dysfunctional Teacher

Cathie West, Principal

"I have encountered numerous troubled teachers throughout my long career, but were there a prize for Most Dysfunctional, Paula, a sixth-grade teacher, would win it hands down. What follows are a few highlights from my exasperating life with Paula and what I learned.

"I had just become principal of the school where Paula taught, and she was the first teacher to visit, in early July. She entered my office like a frightened bird, then sat hunched over on her chair clutching a wad of tissue. In a halting fashion, Paula expressed fear that I had heard bad things about her and she had come to tell her side. 'I was miserable,' Paula complained, dabbing at her eyes with the tissue. 'I tried my best, but every time I turned around, the principal found something wrong. I didn't know what to do—it was awful!' Paula convinced me that all she wanted was a little support and a fresh start, and I readily agreed to help her.

"After she left, I pulled her personnel file and then phoned my predecessor. I learned that two years earlier, she had been a late hire, fresh out of school, who had floundered almost immediately. Paula couldn't pull a lesson together, handle rambunctious students, or keep the parents happy. In the state where I was working, new teachers are on probation for three years before being recommended for a continuing contract or nonrenewal and since this was Paula's third year on probation, we had a lot to accomplish in a very short time.

"I called Paula in to develop a plan. We discussed previous complaints, set goals, and outlined remedies. I said I would visit her often to give her the feedback she needed. Paula was optimistic that she would succeed, and I was rooting for her. But my life with Paula would soon become like that pithy definition of history—'just one damn thing after another.'

"My first visit to Paula's classroom in September was diagnostic. The lesson I observed was confusing, too long, and undeniably boring. Paula's sixth graders reacted in typical preteen fashion—tuning out, fooling around, or openly mocking her. I met with Paula afterward and provided her with a lesson-planning guide, some *no-fail* teaching strategies, and a discipline plan that coupled clear expectations with lots of positive feedback. `I am willing to try anything,' Paula vowed.

"But while Paula struggled to improve her teaching, a succession of blips appeared on my radar screen. In October, I spoke to Paula about her punctuality. She frequently arrived to class just minutes before her students and was often late for recess duty. Paula had excuses for every time she was tardy—her husband had been ill, she was taking an important phone call, or she had a crushing headache. In a woebegone manner, Paula promised to improve. I followed up our meeting with a memo emphasizing that I expected her to arrive on time.

"Then in November, I witnessed a substitute teacher on the phone begging Paula for lesson plans. I was irritated because our policy was clear—sub plans were mandatory, and outlining them by phone was unacceptable. When Paula and I discussed her latest failing, she acted surprised and hurt. `I requested Mrs. Smythe for my sub because she likes to do her own thing. I *never* leave her plans! How was I to know that she would get sick and some other sub would come in her place?' Patiently, I reviewed the policy and documented our meeting with another memo.

"I continued to observe Paula regularly and saw small improvements in her teaching and student management, but both were still marginal and inconsistent. I kept making suggestions, but it was apparent that teaching did not come naturally to Paula.

"In December, a colleague reported that Paula had screamed at her during a discussion about field trip plans. A short time later Paula appeared, looking shaken. She admitted that she had lost her temper and blamed her hysterics on her husband's health problems—he had just learned he was diabetic. `I'll apologize immediately,' Paula promised. `This will never happen again!' I reviewed our staff Behavior Code with her and outlined my expectations in a memo.

"But Paula *did* do it again a few weeks later, only this time via a caustic e-mail that she circulated to other teachers. I was flabbergasted! Was Paula mentally unbalanced? When I confronted her, she explained that all of her ideas for an end-of-year picnic had been opposed, a real slap in the face! Paula admitted that the retaliatory e-mail was a huge mistake, and this time she blamed her lack of judgment on financial problems. Since Paula was contrite, I responded with an oral reprimand.

"Then in January, I was astounded to find a glass jar of scorpions on Paula's desk. A month earlier, after confiscating a black widow from a first grader, I had announced to teachers that toxic creatures were not welcome at our school. When I confronted Paula, she looked crestfallen. `I was just trying to beef up my science lesson,' she explained. Needless to say, the scorpions were sent packing, and it was time to do the same with Paula.

"I made an appointment with the personnel director, and we reviewed Paula's employment history. Her two final evaluations from the previous principal were full of suggestions, but every competency area had been marked satisfactory, so if we recommended nonrenewal, the case against Paula would rest solely upon my work. It was time to get advice from the school district's attorney.

"I knew that probationary teachers at risk for nonrenewal had to be notified by February 15th, but I wasn't sure what documents to prepare. The attorney was a huge help. I was asked to write a midyear performance evaluation that included a recommendation for nonrenewal and also a plan of assistance. Paula would have from mid-February until mid-May, when final evaluations were due, to improve her performance, or the nonrenewal recommendation would become a reality.

"At the performance review meeting, Paula shrieked that I never offered her any help and treated her unfairly. She claimed that other teachers came in late or failed to write sub plans but were ignored because they were my favorites. Then to my surprise, Paula presented letters of support from two teachers. These same teachers had more than once complained that Paula was a washout.

"Then the union representative joined in with accusations of harassment, complaints that I had fuzzy expectations, and doubts about my competence. The representative pointed out that Paula had two years of satisfactory evaluations and wanted to know what my problem was. He demanded that the nonrenewal statement be omitted and the assistance plan withdrawn.

"After several hours of contentious debate that included tearful pleadings from Paula, I brought the meeting to a close—I could not in good conscience agree to their requests. Paula and the representative walked out threatening to go to the school board, which did not surprise me, but what *did* was Paula's resignation the following day.

"Years later, I still think about Paula. Being a principal is hard work, and letting a teacher go makes it even tougher. The time commitment and stress are horrific! But doing the right thing is its own reward."

Case Study: My Volunteer Mission—Rehabilitate David

Cal Miller, Principal

"David was assigned to my school at a district meeting during which a decision was made that he could not continue in his current teaching position. After a very short discussion in which no other principal was willing to accept him, I volunteered. I had a strong staff that I hoped would be a positive influence on him.

"Initially, David's anger was focused on his former colleagues and principal. He accused them of stealing his materials, lying about him, and making his life miserable. His behavior in my school generally and with his students in the classroom was acceptable. He seemed to have put his problems behind him.

"After the first-year honeymoon, his instability started to surface in Year 2. Relationships with his fellow teachers were strained. He would plan something with them and then fail to complete his part of the project. He started to miss days of work, arrive late, and be unprepared for class. His paperwork was usually late. Although his instructional performance during scheduled observations was still acceptable, I noticed his students were often out of control and wasting time when I passed or visited his classroom unannounced.

"We met before school one fall morning to discuss my observations and concerns. He told me that family problems were keeping him awake at night and causing him a great deal of stress. I asked if I could do anything to help. He declined my help. We agreed on the need to have clear lesson plans prepared for each day, just in case his family situation forced him to miss school.

"Three days later, I noticed he was not in his classroom as the children entered the building for the day. I escorted his students into their classroom and called the office to check on him. I stayed in the class for about an hour and fifteen minutes until he arrived. After school, I met with him to discuss his failure to have clear, focused, purposeful plans available for substitutes. He apologized and gave me more information about his situation at home. His fifteen-year-old daughter had fallen in with the wrong crowd, and he was afraid she might be experimenting with drugs. I mentioned the district's EAP and what it might be able to do for his family. He declined any assistance and promised that he would no longer allow his problems at home to interfere with his work.

"Unfortunately, this was a promise he could not keep. Problems at home escalated, and his behavior at work continued to deteriorate. He had a shouting match with a fellow teacher, parents started to report complaints by their children, and my observations documented disorganized lessons and growing discipline referrals.

"It became obvious to me that my meetings with him were doing no good. Every time we met, he would tell me more about the issues at home and promise that they would no longer interfere with his teaching.

"Early in December, I did another formal observation and was very concerned by his lack of preparation and deteriorating classroom control. What had been an organized, productive classroom was now a smoldering powder keg. I asked him to bring the building union representative with him to our postobservation conference. I expected him to be very hostile about what I had written in my observation report. In spite of knowing in advance that I would be in his classroom that morning, his instruction had been a disaster. Children were not paying attention, and he had no idea what or how he planned to control them, let alone teach them, that morning.

"In our conference, we wrote an Individual Development Plan. We agreed that he would use the winter holiday break to prepare a written semester plan for completing instruction of the fifth-grade curriculum. The second goal in his IDP was to develop and incorporate a consistent positive behavior system for his classroom. His final goal was to re-establish positive working relationships with his grade-level team. During the remaining days before the holiday, he was at school on time each day, and his lesson plans were ready in advance.

"I settled back to enjoy my vacation with the hope that the worst of David's problems were behind us. My optimism was in vain. During the first week, he missed two days of work. When he returned to work, he was a wreck. I asked him what I could do to help, and he exploded at me. He said that he was tired of my prying into his private life, that he knew I was out to get him, and that he and the union would take care of me if I didn't leave him alone.

"After this confrontation, I contacted the Director of Elementary Education and gave her the background. I also set up a meeting with David and his union representative and invited another principal to observe. The meeting started out well enough. I laid out my concerns and observations and reviewed the plan we had made in December. I told them that I wanted to add the expectation that David would have to give me his lesson plans one week in advance. I stated that if he made another verbal attack on me or on anyone on school grounds, he would be suspended from work. At this point, he exploded and went into a verbal tirade about all of us being out to get him. He stormed out of the meeting slamming the door. I told the union representative that my expectations stood and that I was issuing a formal written reprimand to David for his behavior in the meeting.

"Three weeks later, I suspended David when he verbally attacked a fifth-grade teacher after she reminded him that it was his turn for recess duty and he was late. David took a medical leave for the rest of the year.

"Regrettably, the real problem was never solved. David could not be helped until he realized that he needed help. My deep regret is that given the purpose of schooling, children in the classes of teachers like David are forced to suffer through months or even years of inadequate teaching. When even one staff member in a school has a serious problem, it can impact everyone in the school. It falls to the principal to recognize potential problems and take steps to alleviate their impact on the school's educational program."

Guidelines for Principals

The troubled teachers in Cathie and Cal's case studies are remarkably similar. Resist the temptation to diagnose, but do consider the following important guidelines as you deal with teachers whose behavior is unpredictable and volatile.

Be Optimistic

Most teachers with possible mental disorders will display some type of inappropriate behavior that must be confronted immediately with AIs. In the case of Paula, she laid her problems at Cathie's doorstep before school even started. David, on the other hand, was able to keep the majority of his problems under control for a whole school year. Both principals dealt immediately with the problems these teachers presented.

If troubled teachers are ready and willing to change after you make your initial AI presentation, sincerely convey your commitment to give them the benefit of the doubt and an opportunity for a fresh start. Both Cathie and Cal exhibited a sense of confidence regarding their own abilities to help these teachers be successful. They also demonstrated a positive outlook regarding the teachers' potential for success. Initially, both teachers responded positively to their principals' leadership, but when in-school and out-of-school stressors increased, their behavior deteriorated.

Document

It's a mistake to think that if things are going relatively well, notes and documentation aren't important. If a teacher is acting erratically or irrationally, document all observations and meetings immediately after they occur. Maintain a diary or computer file in which you record the dates, times, and transcripts of all meetings; the dates, times, and transcripts of all teacher observations; copies of all memos and letters sent to teachers; and transcripts of all conversations with parents, students, and teachers regarding things troubled teachers have said or done. If you take a wait-and-see attitude, you may lose valuable documentation you could need in the future.

Refer

Getting help for troubled teachers, even if they agree to it, can be difficult unless you have an EAP or a well-run community mental health program. Veterans may be eligible for treatment at a local Veterans Administration facility. Districts without formal EAPs may be willing to negotiate specific agreements to pay for mental health services. Never attempt the diagnosis or counseling of troubled teachers yourself. Focus solely on dealing with their inappropriate behaviors as evidenced in the school setting.

Involve Union Representation

In many districts, union representation is mandatory at all meetings to discuss job performance. In others, union representation is only required when you are formally disciplining or not renewing a contract. Maintain a positive and proactive attitude regarding the union's involvement. I experienced a teacher-dismissal process in which the union representative and I worked with our respective constituencies to negotiate a settlement that would allow a teacher with apparent cognitive difficulties to retire. A positive and cooperative attitude toward your district's union leaders or the salaried professionals of the state organization sends the message that you intend to be fair, honest, and professional in your dealings with all teachers and that you welcome observers and advocates at all meetings.

Be Prepared

Be ready for anything. Teachers with mental disorders may become abusive, irrational, aggressive, or even violent. Think ahead about how you will react, what you will say, and what strategies you will use to keep your cool as well as how you will soothe the troubled teacher and minimize the trauma to students and other teachers.

You will at some point be accused, abused, and threatened; count on it. In most cases, the verbiage is designed to intimidate you so you will back off. Remain calm, and consult frequently with central office personnel and the district's legal counsel. Be an assertive administrator. If you have followed all of the appropriate procedures, you have nothing to fear.

Know When to Fold

Reminiscent of the country western song, Cathie and Cal both knew when to hold (keep working with the troubled teachers and giving them one more chance to change) and when to lay their cards on the table and fold (prepare for dismissal). They reached a point of no return with their troubled teachers—the moment at which their optimistic hopes for behavioral change vanished. They decisively moved to the next step—calling in central office and legal counsel to prepare a case for dismissal.

Be Persistent and Consistent

There are hundreds of thousands of troubled teachers who remain in classrooms because no principal has been willing to hold them to a reasonable set of professional expectations and behavior. If ignored, many troubled teachers don't bother anyone except their unfortunate students or an occasional parent who wonders in vain how this kind of behavior can be tolerated in a school. Oh, there may be an occasional incident, but if the principal fails to follow up consistently and persistently, it's business as usual for the troubled teacher.

Once you set forth expectations, monitor performance, and confront troubled teachers with their inappropriate behavior, they often begin to unravel. To their fellow teachers, it may appear as though your harassment is responsible for their behavior. In reality, the troubled teachers are unable to meet acceptable performance standards and fall back on inappropriate behaviors to cover up their incompetence and extricate themselves from the demands you are making.

Don't Give Up

Dealing with troubled teachers is very different from dealing with troubled salespersons or engineers. Oh, there are consequences for productivity in any organization that ignores troubled employees, but troubled teachers spend long periods of time alone with vulnerable and impressionable students. So if you are tempted to ignore your troubled teachers, remember your students and persevere!

HOW TO DEAL WITH TEACHERS
WHO ARE LEGALLY COMPROMISED

There are two ways teachers can be in trouble with the law: (1) breaking a criminal statute or (2) violating the civil rights of someone else, making the school district vulnerable to a civil suit. Dealing with teachers whom you suspect may be breaking the law or violating the civil rights of students, parents, or colleagues is different from dealing with other types of difficult teachers. There are more stringent expectations regarding the reporting of your suspicions, particularly when they involve teachers who are sexually abusing students. In some states, even a casual suspicion that a teacher (or parent) is sexually abusing a student requires the notification of either law enforcement or child protection authorities immediately. District policies will dictate whether you or a superior make that notification. Be certain that you do not cede your legal responsibilities to a central office administrator who fails to follow through or you may find yourself in trouble with the law (Scarpinato, 2004).

There are several things you must do when you have reason to believe a staff member may have committed a criminal act, either on school grounds or outside of school:

- Inform your immediate supervisor. At that point, the entire process may be removed from your jurisdiction. In many states, if you suspect sexual abuse of a student by a teacher, you are legally required to notify the child protection agency in your state immediately. If the reported behavior is sexual harassment, there are no doubt district policies and procedures that apply to a civil rights violation.
- Call the police department to report the crime. You will not want to charge a staff member with a crime until an investigation has been completed.
- If a staff member is about to be (or has been) charged with a crime by the police and your district has a public relations specialist, call that individual.
- If a staff member is about to be (or has been) charged with a crime by the police and your district has a personnel director, call that individual also.

Of course, removing troubled teachers from classrooms, even those charged and convicted of criminal misconduct, ultimately depends on whether your superintendent and school board will support you and provide ongoing legal counsel regarding what to do and say. One of the most appalling cases I have seen of union intimidation and failure to face reality involved a charismatic teacher in a suburban midwestern high school. He hung on to his job for more than a decade in spite of multiple administrative and student complaints regarding inappropriate behavior (drinking alcohol at a student party), sexual harassment of at least one student and one teacher, habitual tardiness, three DUI arrests and convictions, and a court appearance under the influence of alcohol. It appeared to those who watched the story unfold in the newspapers that the central office administration and school board were afraid of the union *and* embarrassed about this blot on the reputation of their flagship high school. The teacher in question had served as both union president and chief negotiator for many years. Only after he received his third conviction for drunken driving and appeared before the judge during sentencing under the influence of alcohol did the school board *finally* vote to dismiss him.

When *any* individual or group, whether building principal, central office administrator, or school board, subscribes to the "don't ask, don't tell" theory of supervision, they make it all the more difficult for those who follow to do the right thing. The cost of ignoring troubled teachers, especially when their behavior is illegal, is catastrophic for students.

Unfortunately, in many communities, protecting the reputation of the district, school board members, and current and former administrators often takes precedence over protecting students and upholding the law (Morales, 2004; Tapia, 1997). The following brief case study illustrates how easily the culture of a school or entire district can succumb to supporting teachers rather than students. The author is currently a high school principal who wishes to remain anonymous.

Case Study: Making Waves: Confronting an Unhealthy School Culture

"I was the new kid on the block—twenty-eight years old, a strong feminist, and the assistant principal of one of the most elite comprehensive high schools in the state. All of the other administrators had been at the school for years. Even though I was young to be an administrator, I wasn't a babe in the woods. I was well connected in town and on a first-name basis with the county attorney and law enforcement personnel because of my involvement in setting up a rape crisis center in town. So when I told my principal that I had good reason to suspect the chorus teacher of sodomizing boys in his office and he told me not to report it, I ignored him. I knew that if the information I had received were substantiated in an investigation, the teacher would be convicted of a crime.

"I went to the County Attorney who felt my information was credible. He selected several detectives from the police department to start interviewing male choir students. The investigators found fifteen victims who were willing to make statements and testify, but the police estimated there were a hundred or more victims. Ten months passed from the day I gave my information to the county attorney until the chorus teacher was dismissed.

"During that same period of time, a group of students came to me to complain about the girls' basketball coach. They told me he was having sexual intercourse with members of the team. This time, I bypassed my principal and went straight to the county attorney who investigated the allegations. At a special school board meeting convened to ask for the teacher's resignation, he repeatedly denied that he was guilty until several of his victims were invited into the meeting to confront him. He immediately resigned and left the state.

"After these two incidents, the principal seldom spoke to me again. I was transferred out of the building and accused of giving the school a bad name. What a shame that professional educators are willing to sacrifice children to protect their image."

SUMMING UP

The "big ideas" of this chapter require character to implement:

- To deal with teachers who are temporarily troubled, be supportive and empathetic, but continue to communicate high expectations and focus teachers' attention on the needs of students. Don't feel so sorry for troubled teachers that you give them permission to exhibit unprofessional behavior. Remember, they are teachers, and the needs of their students take precedence over their troubles!

- Dealing with teachers who exhibit symptoms consistent with mental disorders is a challenge that can only be met with persistence, consistency, and an overriding desire to protect vulnerable students.
- Dealing with teachers who are suspected of criminal misconduct requires fortitude, a tough skin, and a strong sense of moral outrage. These teachers are abusing their positions of trust. You won't get any awards for blowing the whistle, but you will rest easier when you reflect on the students you have protected.

Strategies for Dealing With Exhausted, Stressed, or Burned-Out Teachers

Before you begin Chapter 5 . . .

Bear in mind this advice:

One of the most important and positive things we can give others is hope with direction, encouragement, and believability—hope that the future is going to be bright for them, regardless of where they are at the moment.

—Ziglar (1986, p. 213)

Why do teachers burn out? The answers vary: broken promises, fear of failure, a shortfall of resources, abusive or inconsistent leadership, a pervasive sense of "been there, done that," or a serious case of impossibility thinking. Many of our country's most demoralized teachers work in massive urban districts where low-performing students and failing schools are now making headlines. Who can blame these teachers for feeling burned out?

A PRINCIPAL'S PERSPECTIVE

Principal Ron Collins spent four years on loan from his district working to energize and revitalize urban schools. He explains why, in his opinion, there are so many burned-out teachers in big city systems:

> Like most of us, these teachers came into the profession to help children learn. During their tenure in some very difficult situations, they have not experienced as much success as they expected. At the same time, they are being bombarded with media reports about their "failures," faced with systemic inconsistencies, central office shifts in emphasis, as well as frequent changes in building leadership. The majority of "burned-out" teachers display symptoms of "learned helplessness." They no longer believe that their efforts can impact progress toward the goal for all children to achieve at grade level. They have descended into the blame game. They blame their students, the parents, the community, their administrator, the district, the State Department of Education, and politicians. In their more reflective moments, they blame themselves and question if they should continue in the profession.

There are undeniable challenges to teaching in urban settings, but teachers in suburban schools are burning out as well. This chapter's case study describes an entire faculty that is worn to a frazzle: twenty teachers at the Sunny Skies Elementary School located in a Midwestern suburban school district. Their story is told from two perspectives: (1) the principal's description of her faculty's exhaustion and (2) one faculty member's perception of why she and her colleagues are so demoralized. (Note: The names of the school and district have been changed to protect the privacy of staff members.)

Case Study 1: The Principal's Perspective: Twenty Teachers Worn to a Frazzle

"I believe that all twenty of my teachers are continually stressed and fatigued. The demands of the district, combined with the state and national mandates, keep the learning curve vertical. There is too little time to implement anything well. Today's children bring so many social challenges to the classroom along with the inevitable inappropriate and uncooperative behaviors, to say nothing of the learning difficulties, that there never seem to be enough services to help them. Their parents are often unavailable for meaningful involvement. These challenges complicate the act of teaching and drain teachers' energies.

"I think there are so many tired teachers because the demands for accountability have increased dramatically. Meanwhile, the social climate of our society is reflected in the increased number of troubled children we see in our classrooms. The teachers need more social support to help these children become mentally and physically available for learning.

"I do whatever I can to lighten my teachers' load. I try to screen the information and tasks to eliminate some of the overload. I structure assignments with very specific expectations and directions. I make time available in the school day for collaboration, planning, and curriculum development. I encourage teachers to follow their dreams and hunches. I praise and recognize teachers regularly.

"But central office increases its demands without ever eliminating anything from our plates. Also, we are often told what to do without being taught how to do it. Teacher exhaustion creates a depressing atmosphere that results in negative reactions whenever new ideas or programs are suggested. There is an attitude, even among some of the best teachers, that screams, 'Don't ask any more of me!' How can we address the issues of NCLB (No Child Left Behind Act) and our district's demands without overwhelming our excellent teachers? How can I support my teachers as they deal with the social and learning disabilities presented by their students?"

You can hear the frustration in this principal's lament. What's the solution for these twenty exhausted teachers? As you may already have surmised, dealing with an entire faculty of tired teachers requires more than AIs. Oh, it might be appropriate for a particular teacher who has become the self-appointed "spokesperson in charge of complaining," but when *everyone* is down in the dumps, more systemic initiatives are needed.

God grant [us] the serenity to accept the things [we] cannot change; the courage to change the things [we] can; and the wisdom to know the difference.

Traditional German prayer, translated by Reinhold Niebuhr

Management and leadership guru, Peter Drucker (as quoted in Covey, 1989, p. 154), says, "Effective people are not problem-minded; they're opportunity minded." In the spirit of Drucker's statement, after exploring the presenting problems that appear to be the source of exhaustion at Sunny Skies, I will suggest some opportunities for rejuvenation.

The goal of this chapter is to help the principal of Sunny Skies (and you) to deal productively with exhausted teachers. To do that, we will focus on several key principles regarding individual and organizational energy:

- Energy for work comes from a variety of inner resources and must be used wisely and renewed and recovered periodically.
- A variety of factors can sap energy in the workplace but the most insidious is lack of purpose and meaning.
- Among the four categories of exhausted teachers discussed later in the chapter, those who are demoralized by a sense of diminished freedom in an age of accountability and results impact the culture of their schools most negatively.
- Administrators, both building-level and central office, may unknowingly contribute to exhaustion among teachers.
- Personal *and* organizational energy can be restored and revived by renewing the sense of corporate purpose, revisiting the school mission, and paying attention to critical culture issues which may remain unspoken and unexplored.

SOURCES OF ENERGY

Energy for work, whatever the job, is a resource that must be used wisely and renewed periodically. The energy to work at the same job passionately, day in and day out, with a high level of productivity, whether it's teaching five-year-olds or mopping the cafeteria, comes from a variety of sources:

- Commitment to a cause and a purpose
- Success in reaching a worthy mission
- Affirmation from coworkers, supervisors, or "clients"
- A sense of teamwork and community, pulling together against the odds
- Intrinsic motivation
- Making a difference in the lives of others
- Eating properly, exercising regularly, and getting enough sleep
- Taking time for recovery, celebration, and reflection
- Taking responsibility for one's own emotions and actions

Eddie Brown was my head custodian for several years. At the age of 70, he was able to work longer, harder, and with more enthusiasm than almost anyone on my staff. He kept the school in white-glove condition and at a moment's notice could coax our 100-year-old boiler back to working order or shovel three feet of new-fallen snow off the front walk.

Eddie's energy seemed boundless, but his fountain of youth flowed from several important sources. His *cause* and *mission* were focused on having the best-looking school facility in the district. Despite the fact that our building was the oldest, it was also the cleanest and best maintained. He consistently received top ratings from his central office supervisor as well as compliments from teachers and parents, *affirmation* that his work was noticed and appreciated. He believed that, to learn, students needed a clean and safe environment. He took great *pride in being part of the school team* that was raising achievement year after year. Not only did he clean and maintain the building, he also *made a difference in people's lives*, mentoring the high school students who worked for him as sweepers, encouraging teachers who were going through tough times, and cheering on students who suddenly discovered how much fun work could be.

Eddie wasn't a workaholic, however. Every weekend, he and his "bride" of nearly five decades took their camper and went fishing. He was able to work with purpose and vision long past the time when most of his peers had turned in their keys because he knew the importance of *recovery and reflection.* One of the things I admired most about Eddie Brown was that he was an independent thinker. He knew the importance of *taking responsibility for his own actions.* If he disagreed with the prevailing opinion among his peers, he had no hesitation to take a stand, and if he thought something was wrong, he didn't do it. He said what was on his mind but always politely and respectfully.

> To the degree that leaders and managers build cultures around continuous work—whether that means several-hour meetings, or long days, or the expectation that people will work in the evenings and on weekends—performance is necessarily compromised over time.
>
> **—Loehr and Schwartz (2003, p. 30)**

FACTORS THAT SAP PERSONAL ENERGY

Energy for work is generally a renewable resource (given the proper attention to rest, rejuvenation, and bodily nourishment), but irrespective of job roles, there are a variety of factors that can sap personal energy to the point of exhaustion:

- Ceding important decisions to others
- Blaming others for the way we feel
- Feeling that our security and survival are at risk
- Lack of structure, routines, and rituals in our work or personal lives
- Anxiety and fear
- Eating the wrong things
- Being physically out of shape
- Having a sense of failure
- Feeling a lack of control over decisions
- Sleep deprivation and illness

- Feeling unknowledgeable or unprepared
- Working without a vision
- Allowing others to define our purpose
- Putting in time without seeing results
- Living a lie: being dishonest with ourselves
- Living with lies: dishonesty on the part of others

CHARACTERISTICS OF EXHAUSTED TEACHERS

There are three categories of teachers who present exhaustion and stress as symptoms:

1. Highly frustrated teachers who have lost any sense of efficacy they once had and feel they no longer have control over what happens to them anymore

2. Genuinely overworked teachers whose schools are understaffed and poorly funded

3. Deeply troubled teachers whose apparent exhaustion may in reality be the result of temporary personal troubles or depression

There is a fourth category of teachers who occasionally *seem* to be exhausted but in reality are creative and high-energy "workaholics" who thrive on balancing multiple projects and view stress as a normal part of life rather than as a problem. According to a psychologist who has studied these types of workers, they are high in hardiness and enjoy ongoing changes and difficulties. The tougher the work gets, the more involved they become (O'Connor, 2004).

In our teacher case study, a faculty member at Sunny Skies shares her perspective regarding the problems that are demoralizing her colleagues. She puts her finger on a unique energy source not always recognized or understood by administrators: the freedom to choose what, how, and when to teach without being tied to a specific curriculum, methodology, or prescription.

The perception of many teachers that *they* are rightfully the final arbiters of what students should learn and how best to teach it offers one explanation regarding why the Sunny Skies teachers are feeling so downtrodden. The educational paradigm that has guided their thinking for decades has recently changed dramatically. It has shifted from a focus on activity to a demand for achievement, from fun to accountability, and from academic freedom to prescribed outcomes and assessments. Fighting what they perceive to be a disastrous transition is wearing many teachers to a frazzle. Feelings of anxiety, fear, lack of control, and failure are taking their toll. Here's how the Sunny Skies teacher described what is happening.

Case Study 2: A Teacher's Perspective: Stress and More Stress

"I see the Annual Yearly Progress (AYP) requirement of the NCLB as the most stressful thing for teachers to bear right now. Most teachers feel accountable for what they do and believe that assessment is necessary to track student growth and to help determine programming. But in a district like Meadow Glen, we've always been about that. However, when a school fails one year because of a small percentage of students and a few uncontrollable variables, it is very distressing. We are working incredibly hard, and some of these students still can't read on grade level. We don't know what else to do. This is unbelievably stressful, and stress saps energy.

"Another major problem that is wearing us out is student behavior. This is my sixteenth year of teaching, and I have seen student behavior change quite a lot over the years. So many kids, as well as their parents, have very little respect for teachers. We have become rather powerless when it comes to classroom discipline. When I was in school, even if my teachers were wrong, my parents said they were right. It's not that way anymore.

"Difficult parents are another factor sapping our energies. Many parents still do not get the idea that they are ultimately responsible for their children's education. We are with the students only five and a half hours of a day, for only nine months out of the year. Education has to start at home. Nothing is more frustrating for a teacher who works hard to promote good learning habits at school to discover that there is no follow-through at home.

"Negative staff morale is another real energy-zapper. It is very tiring to hear colleagues complain constantly about things like endless paperwork, too many unproductive meetings, too many committees, and other things that never seem to change.

"But what really wears us thin is just plain having too much to do. Because we are a very small school in a suburban district with many larger schools, every staff member has to serve on at least four committees. We are stretched far too thin. There is too much time spent at home on lesson planning and grading because our planning time at school is tied up with committee work.

"Then, our curriculum is overloaded. Every subject has its own central office specialist, and each one has an idea of what should be covered in a specific subject. If you add everything up, there's too much to fit in during the available time. Since we have to cover every word in the curriculum for every subject, there simply isn't time to do anything fun anymore. I am a support teacher and haven't taught in the regular classroom for seven years. If I went back into the classroom and taught like I did when I left, I would not be considered a good teacher, at least not in the Meadow Glen District. I used to do class plays, creative centers, unit studies, and projects. Now, if it isn't curriculum driven, forget it.

"The worst energy-eater, however, is blame. When teachers are the ones held responsible for low achievement, it saps our energy like nothing else. I honestly believe that is how the majority of the teachers on our staff feel. I often wonder why we all stick with it. I guess that being dedicated to children and the field of teaching is what enables us to carry on."

Principals' Roundtable: Dealing With Exhausted Teachers

Elaine: I'm surprised that there aren't more exhausted teachers out there, given the physical and emotional demands of the job.

Doug Pierson: Teaching is undeniably a hard job, and after ten months of doing it, most of us are exhausted. The percentage of exhausted teachers in my school is always lower in September.

Elaine: Why do some teachers get exhausted and others don't?

Sue Braithwaite: Some teachers do have bigger workloads than others. I have several exhausted teachers this year. Some of them are dual-language-immersion bilingual teachers who feel they are doing twice as much work as most other teachers because they share students with other teachers and have sixty instead of thirty every day. They spend more time communicating with their teammates and parents to make sure there is a seamless transition between classes. The second group of exhausted teachers has an overload of students with severe behavior problems in their classrooms.

Elaine: How have you helped these teachers who are genuinely tired?

Sue Braithwaite: I gave them additional team planning time (with substitutes) so that they could catch up on student evaluations, team collaboration, and parent contacts. I believe they felt validated and appreciated having this extra time. I did this four times throughout the year. And then, I just listened to their concerns.

Cathie West: My exhausted teachers have a difficult time setting limits for themselves. They have benefited from AIs that confront them with the fact that they are getting carried away with too many commitments. Sometimes, they just need to be reminded.

Todd Lambert: I do have more teachers in the exhausted category than in any of the others. I think this is because there is a great deal of pressure for my teachers to succeed. Most of our parents have achieved financial success because of their educational efforts. They want their children to go at least one step farther than they have gone, so the pressure gets pretty intense for teachers, especially if they aren't prepared for it.

Elaine: What have you done to help teachers with this pressure from the parents?

Todd Lambert: I've relieved them of some of the extra duties that are expected. However, after four years as a building principal, I've learned that some people will always pile on responsibilities for themselves. I don't know if it's their inability to say no, or if additional responsibilities give them a sense of control or self-worth. I do know that it usually doesn't work to take things off their plates.

Jim Ratledge: Although I don't currently have any exhausted teachers, I did have one staff member who had some medical issues, and we worked out a job share with a new mom on the staff that was advantageous to everyone, especially the students.

Kathy Johnson: My tired teacher had more parent complaints and had a rougher time handling problem students. I gave her some aide time and asked that she include me in her parent meetings at first so I could see what was going wrong in her discussions. Her demeanor was very downtrodden, and it was hard for her to think of interventions and solutions. She did get better as the year progressed.

Shirley Johnson: My burned-out teachers are crabby and wired too tight. They complain about the least little thing. So I plan ahead for them. I make sure that when there are issues that I know will bother them, I solve the problems ahead of time. This keeps me on my toes, but it keeps them from ragging to other teachers.

Elaine: Shirley is talking about an aspect of "exhaustion" that really doesn't have to do with being overworked so much as being discouraged and depressed about the results of hard work or being upset with the people with whom we're working—low morale.

Corinne Archie-Edwards: I find that when there is an overall commitment to the work that we're doing, it overrides any problems we encounter that might lower morale. However, there are times when morale is momentarily affected because of a lack of 100% cooperation. At times like these, I have focused on listening more and have learned the value of staying in tune with the underground communication systems in the building. We regroup and provide opportunities for staff celebration and camaraderie. It seems to help.

Elaine: You've hit on the "big idea" of this chapter, Corinne—the importance of being focused as a team on a worthwhile goal and then taking time out for celebration and renewal once a goal has been reached.

HOW ADMINISTRATORS SAP THEIR TEACHERS' ENERGIES

Although I love to walk, I dislike treadmills. I may burn up a calorie or two, but I never get anywhere. It's a problem in schools as well. Administrators at every level need to examine whether they are depleting their teachers' energies with programs, policies, and procedures that keep everyone on a treadmill but rarely advance the school's mission. Consider the following examples.

> People's attitudes toward their jobs and the degree to which they feel they make a difference by showing up each day have long been considered powerful indicators of how well they will do. Being just another cog in a machine with no say over what happens is almost guaranteed to cause burnout. But even in the most grueling work environment, people can cope if they feel they have some control.
>
> —O'Connor (2004)

We Forget Who Does the Real Work

This problem is epidemic in larger districts where several layers of central office administration continually invent committees, projects, training, and initiatives for teachers to implement, with little regard for who does the real work in schools. I was hired to present a workshop on instructional leadership to principals of low-performing schools. The folks at the front of the room were energetic, focused, and highly motivated. They were an impressive group of leaders. The folks at the back of the room were huddled around two round tables talking to each other, doing paperwork, and generally being disruptive. I was curious about who these folks were and during the first break made my way to the back of the room.

"How long have you been a principal?" I asked one individual.

"Oh," she responded with a smug smile, "I'm not a principal; I'm a central office administrator."

"Are all of you from central office?" I asked, pointing to the rest of the group.

"Yes, we're in charge of curriculum, staff development, and special projects."

I immediately knew at least *one* reason why so many of the schools in the district were low-performing: A cadre of central office administrators had forgotten who does the real work.

Ron Collins summarized the problem this way:

These teachers have been inserviced and "helped" almost beyond endurance. Strategies and programs have been offered and implemented continuously, but few have been given the support and time necessary to see improvement. Teachers see programs come and go and are no longer willing to invest time in the latest solution. Change has not been developed from the bottom up, and it has not been supported by systemic changes in the system. New programs cannot flourish in the same old system of bureaucratic rules and regulations. These teachers need to be nurtured and given the time to reflect, discuss, and share their views of reality and possible improvements.

We Don't Respect Teachers' Time

There's something magical about the terms *collaboration* and *teamwork* to many administrators, especially those in central office. But as Little (1989) points out, getting everybody into the act for every decision or project can actually slow down or even derail a change effort.

I recently made a presentation to a group organizing a collaborative effort between a university, a school district, and a grant-funded initiative. Their goal is to raise achievement in low-performing schools. Over two days, nearly eighty classroom teacher hours (i.e., number of teachers in attendance times the number of hours spent) were devoted to deliberation over an implementation plan. For teachers who desperately needed help with effective instructional methodologies for at-risk students, it seemed a sad waste of their time. Those in charge could have conferred and made recommendations, and the teachers would have been pleased to work on meaningful lesson plans. Fullan (1991, 1998) points out that endless meetings and overelaborate planning sessions often confuse and alienate participants. Teachers are burned out before they get to implement.

We Expect Lifetime Commitments

Here's how one teacher described this problem: "My colleagues and I have very creative ideas of things we would like to try, but are hesitant to volunteer because once the activity is successful, it can turn into a 'lifetime sentence.' For example, three years ago, I had an idea of doing a Family Night at a local attraction. We had a great turnout and it was a lot of fun. Now I'm expected to manage it every year. I enjoyed doing it once, but when you are told to do something that was your own idea in the first place, the personal satisfaction diminishes."

We Focus on Wood Gathering Rather Than Sea Gazing

If you approach accomplishing a goal (e.g., ensuring that all students are successful) solely in terms of what teachers must "do," chances are they *will* feel overloaded and exhausted. Rather, give them a vision of what can be and an explicit mission to accomplish that vision, and you will find them re-energized for what lies ahead. Antoine de Saint-Exupéry (1950) advised, "If you want to build a ship, don't gather your people and ask them to provide wood, prepare tools, assign tasks. Call them together and raise in their minds the longing for the endless sea."

We Don't Finish What We Start

In preparation for this book, I talked to several of my former teachers, asking what, for them, had been most energizing about our school. One teacher warmed my heart as she described the way that we worked on finishing what we started:

> An aspect of our school that I found energizing was our new focus each year. We always had one primary focus for the school year, and we worked together as a staff to address it. Doing so, we came up with some delightful ways to motivate students and staff to work toward the goal. We didn't try to do too much at once or simply drop the previous year's focus as unimportant after we reached our goal. Rather, we incorporated what we had accomplished and continued to move ahead, which made each year feel as though it was built upon a solid foundation that would enable us to reach even higher goals.

HOW TO DEAL WITH AN EXHAUSTED SCHOOL

If, after reading to this point in the chapter, you feel that your school may be suffering from overall exhaustion and stress compounded by a serious case of impossibility thinking, there are several things you can do. First, recognize that "great leaders are the stewards of organizational energy" (Loehr & Schwartz, 2003, p. 17). It will take more than a pep talk and donuts to revitalize your teachers. Only an examination of and rededication to what's really important can provide the energy that is needed to accomplish your mission. There are a variety of ways to do this, but only you can decide which of the following recommendations to implement.

Assume Nothing

Don't assume that you know all of the reasons for exhaustion among your staff members until you have invited them to speak honestly about what they perceive the problems to be. For example, here's what one teacher said in response to Indicator 4 of The Healthy School Checklist: *The principal encourages open communication among staff members and parents and maintains respect for differences of opinion*:

> The leader must have an infectious optimism and the determination to persevere in the face of difficulties. . . . The final test of a leader is the feeling you have when you leave his presence after a conference. Have you a feeling of uplift and confidence?
>
> —Montgomery (1961, pp. 13–14)

We are often asked to share our ideas and opinions, but sometimes there is a feeling among the staff that it is better not to respond. Sometimes we feel if we don't give the response that is being sought or if we deliver our opinions the wrong way, we may not be looked upon very favorably. Does that make sense? I can't put my finger on the exact reason why we feel like this. It is just that no one ever wants to cause any waves. No one wants to put their neck on the chopping block, so to speak, so a lot of times we don't share what we're really thinking, even when we are given the opportunity to do so.

There are many ways to find out if you have a similar problem with communication in your school: (1) Have teachers meet in small groups similar to parking-lot meetings, (2) ask teachers to complete a survey like the Healthy School Checklist, (3) give teachers the opportunity to evaluate your job performance using the Ten Traits of Highly Effective Principals evaluation, or (4) hire an independent consultant to do a building audit. The assessments and processes just mentioned can be found in The Culture Builder's Toolkit (Resource B).

Prioritize

Goethe advised, "Things which matter most must never be at the mercy of things which matter least." If you become bogged down in the minutia "buses, budgets, and boilers," you will lose sight of what is most important—teaching and learning. Renew your commitment to the things which matter most daily.

Confront Impossibility Thinking

Have you ever looked at yourself in an antique mirror and immediately realized that you weren't looking at the real you, but a distorted image? The same phenomenon occurs in teachers' minds as they hold up the challenges of leaving no child behind to the mirror of impossibility thinking. Their thinking has become distorted by the way things used to be.

Whenever you hear teachers making statements like those found in the first column of Figure 5.1, jot them down. Once you've collected some of the best statements, create an exercise in which you ask teachers to first translate the statements you've heard them make into what their statements really mean (second column). Then ask them to reframe their statements into possibilities (third column).

Be an Activator

If you've read *The Ten Traits of Highly Effective Principals* (McEwan, 2003), you already know what an activator looks like: a principal filled with zip, gumption, drive, motivation, enthusiasm, energy, spunk, and humor enough to spare and share with staff, parents, and students. "A person filled with gumption doesn't sit around dissipating and stewing about things. He's [she's] at the front of the train of his [her] own awareness, watching to see what's up the track and meeting it when it comes. That's gumption" (Pirsig, 1974, p. 303). Activators take risks, are playful, and have fun while they work.

Figure 5.1 Impossibility Thinking

The Exhausted Educator Says . . .	The Impossibility Thinker Says . . .	The Empowered Educator Says . . .
Parents still do not get the idea that they are ultimately responsible for their children's education.	If parents aren't responsible, it's impossible for me to make a difference in a child's life.	We can make a huge difference in children's lives. Look at what we've already accomplished. Even uncooperative parents are doing the best they can. Maybe if we encouraged and praised them more instead of constantly calling to complain about them and their kids, they would feel more positive. Let's make five positive phone calls a month to our most uncooperative parents.
Since we have to cover every word in the curriculum for every subject, there simply isn't time for anything fun anymore.	It's impossible to create exciting and interesting lessons that teach to the required curricular outcomes.	Of course it's possible to create exciting and interesting lessons that teach important curricular outcomes. Let's use our planning time to design a lesson on summarizing.
When teachers are the ones held responsible for low achievement, it destroys our morale.	It's impossible for me to make a difference in the lives of at-risk students.	I'm responsible for my students' achievement, but I don't have to do it alone. When we work together, anything is possible.
There is too little time to implement anything well. There are never enough services to meet the needs of students. Our society is creating too many troubled children.	It's impossible to reach our mission. There are too many overwhelming problems in today's world.	Anything is possible if we focus our energies on the variables we can control: the time we spend, how we teach, the curriculum we use, the expectations we have for students, and the support we give each other.
We have become rather powerless in the classroom.	It's impossible to have a classroom in which students are well-behaved, on-task, and learning.	If every teacher on the faculty agreed to teach some basic character traits and we combined that with a behavior plan that emphasized rewards for positive behavior and student achievement, I bet we could get our school back on track very quickly.

If you are going to lead your teachers out of their doldrums, you may need to activate the outgoing side of your personality. If you don't consider yourself to be a highly demonstrative individual, your faculty will be all the more motivated to stop whining and get to work if you announce that you will be jumping into a swimming pool with all of your clothes on as soon as all of the kindergarteners can read. Rent the YMCA pool for a Faculty–Family Fun Night and do your thing. Mobilize your entire school (teachers, students, and parents) to help the kindergarten teachers get the job done. After all, every teacher at every grade level will reap the benefits of their success, and older students will also become more fluent readers and increase their vocabulary from reading aloud to their kindergarten buddies.

Flying Solo Has Got to Go

When I began teaching, it was a solitary life. There were no grade-level outcomes or team meetings. I was on my own. If your teachers are still flying solo, it's a surefire way to crash and burnout. Raising student achievement and meeting AYP goals takes collaboration and teamwork. Duets, trios, and quartets are in. Solos are out. Help your teachers to build solid grade-level teams. Use The Team-Builder's Checklist in the Culture Builder's Toolkit to raise their awareness regarding how teams should act and look. Expect teachers to use the words *we, our,* and *us,* rather than *I* and *me,* and model teamwork for them as you talk about your school.

Listen

When you encounter exhaustion resulting from dissension and lack of vision among faculty members, use the Force Field Analysis process (found in The Culture Builder's Toolkit) to identify specific problems that are keeping your school from being a healthy and energized community. If your staff pinpoints the fact that you don't respect their time, take steps to redesign your meetings to include only those items that focus on raising student achievement. If your teachers feel that you're not as open and responsive as you think you are, listen to their suggestions about how you need to change.

Affirm and Reward Yeasayers

Yeasayers are the opposite of naysayers. A naysayer is negative and nitpicky. A yeasayer is optimistic and buoyant. There will always be disasters and downsides in schools (and life). Referenda will fail. Budgets will be cut. But a yeasayer doesn't let momentary bumps in the road interfere with reaching the goal. Identify the yeasayers in your school. Give them perks. Affirm their attitudes. Make them feel that being positive is rewarding and rewarded!

Envision

If you and your teachers have not revisited your school's mission statement in the past three years, or if you have never worked with your current staff to develop a mission statement that reflects *your* vision and values, now is the time to do it. If you don't know where you are going, chances are your faculty won't get there on their own. The development of a new mission statement can bring focus and direction to a group. As Kouzes and Posner (1999) comment, "[Teachers] really do want to make commitments and unite in a common cause where they can accomplish extraordinary things. Great leaders . . . create meaning" (p. 59).

Confront Central Office

If central office is standing in the way of achieving your mission, join with other administrators and conduct AIs with your superintendent or the administrative cabinet. The very thought of a high-risk venture like this might terrify you, but there is safety in numbers. Plan your strategy; keep your list of demands short and powerful. Besides, you may be surprised at how much clout you have when you remind them who is doing the real work of schools!

Encourage

My granddaughter, Elizabeth, and I love the word *perky*. She loves perky people, whether they are servers in restaurants or teachers at school. Perky people are upbeat, energetic, and positive. They make you feel important; they encourage and energize you. If you want your teachers to be perky, you will have to model perkiness for them. In their book, *Encouraging the Heart: A Leader's Guide to Rewarding and Recognizing Others,* Kouzes and Posner (1999) include a twenty-one-item Encouragement Index. Among my favorites are these:

- I express high expectations about what people are capable of accomplishing.
- I make certain we set a standard that motivates us to do better in the future than we are doing now.
- I clearly communicate my personal values and professional standards to everyone on the team.
- I express a positive and optimistic outlook even when times are tough.
- I find ways to make the workplace enjoyable and fun.

Be Confident

Harvard Business School Professor Rosabeth Moss Kanter (2004) suggests that confidence, whether in the members of a basketball team or the employees of an airline, often stands between success and failure. Her research shows that confidence is a capability that can be nurtured by leadership in an organization. Your confidence, the belief that along with your staff you can overcome any obstacles, roadblocks, or detours in the achievement of the mission, can be an ongoing source of inspiration for your teachers.

Reflect

A serious personal illness or family tragedy often compels us to revisit our priorities. Exhaustion in a school should force you to do the same thing. Loehr and Schwartz (2003) suggest the following questions as a good place to start. Ask staff members to first answer them individually and then gather in small groups to share their answers:

- Jump ahead to the end of your life. What are the three most important lessons you have learned, and why are they so critical?
- Think of someone that you deeply respect. Describe three qualities in this person that you most admire.
- Who are you at your best?
- What one-sentence inscription would you like to see on your tombstone that would capture who you really were in your life? (p. 141).

Clean House

Clifton and Nelson (1992) suggest that stress doesn't come from overwork; it's the result of working at a job for which one is totally unsuited. They identify eight weaknesses that appear to be burnout from overwork but are actually indicators of an inability to do the job at all. I've added the italicized explanatory comments that refer specifically to teaching.

- Defensiveness about one's performance: *blaming low achievement on students or parents*
- Obsessive behavior: *worrying over trivial things like bulletin boards, name tags, and bean bag chairs that have nothing to do with teaching and learning*
- Slow learning: *inability to get a concept no matter how many institutes and workshops are attended*
- Lack of profit from repeated experience: *making the same mistakes over and over again with students, parents, and colleagues*
- Lack of automaticity and flow in teaching: *never reaching the point of mastery in classroom management, lesson planning, or lesson delivery*
- Reduced confidence from work: *feeling depressed, unmotivated, disinterested, and even sick after teaching rather than energized*

- Lack of futuristic thinking: *the inability to be reflective and metacognitive about teaching*
- Burnout: a profound and constant sense of failure (adapted from Clifton & Nelson, 1992, pp. 76–84).

Perhaps it's time to do AIs with the teachers you perceive as burned out and confront them with their inability to do the job at all.

Squeeze the Lemons

Renewing a totally burned-out faculty is challenging but not impossible. It takes an individual who regularly practices the seven habits described in Chapter 1 and who is zeroed in like a laser on the mission of the school. My former colleague, Phyllis O'Connell, fits this description to a T. From the moment she took over a low-achieving school with a demoralized faculty, she knew that it would take more than good intentions to refocus her faculty on student learning. First, she hired a consultant who conducted a building audit to squeeze out the key issues that were standing in the way of the school's mission. Phyllis then followed up with team-building activities focused on the problems identified during the consultant's interviews. She says, "My plan was to empower the faculty and teach them how to participate productively in decision making, thereby motivating and energizing them."

Thereafter, whenever morale dipped or teachers turned touchy, she used the Lemon Squeeze process to identify the problem. Phyllis' technique is the perfect one for squeezing out the reasons behind your school's exhaustion. She recommends using either a Force-Field Analysis or an Apollo Process to elicit feedback from people about the issues that are turning them off to effective teaching. See the Culture Builder's Toolkit for the directions and forms you need to use these processes with your teachers. Once you've identified the most important problems, then you can develop a plan with your teachers to solve them. (Note: Phyllis's Lemon Squeeze has no relationship to the "dance of the lemons" discussed in Chapter 6.)

SUMMING UP

Here are the "big ideas" of Chapter 5:

- One way to change teachers' behaviors is to change your own: Make sure that you're part of the solution, not part of the problem.
- Identify the compelling cause to which every teacher can commit, be an instructional resource for your teachers, and together, achieve your goal.
- Do away with impossibility thinking if you want to wipe out exhaustion, raise morale, and energize your faculty.
- Examine what you and your central office administrators may be doing to create exhaustion among teachers and take steps to honor the time and energy of those who are doing the real work of education.
- Tap the power of shared problem solving and decision making to find the source of your teachers' exhaustion as well as to renew their enthusiasm for leaving no child behind.

Strategies for Dealing With Confused, Marginal, or Just Plain Incompetent Teachers

As you read this chapter . . .

Reflect on this wise counsel:

Conflict avoidance in the face of poor performance is an act of moral neglect.

—Fullan (2003, p. 32)

Every spring, college basketball fans around the country look forward to what is known as "the big dance"— the NCAA basketball tournament. This dance starts with sixty-five teams on the "floor," the "partners" who will play each other in an attempt to reach the Final Four. (Note: Basketball purists will quickly point out that the dance starts with sixty-five teams, two of which play each other to narrow the field to sixty-four.) As riveting as this dance always is, it doesn't compare either in size or significance to another eagerly anticipated spring dance—"the dance of the lemons."

The "lemons" are dysfunctional teachers, and this dance pairs them with new principals in different schools. Some of the transfers are voluntary, attempts by teachers to escape impending remediation or possible dismissal. In many cases, principals trade lemons with colleagues, hoping to get slightly more competent or less angry teachers in exchange for their difficult ones. In some cases, changing partners *does* revitalize and renew angry and exhausted teachers, especially if they are reassigned to schools with positive cultures. Unfortunately, however, marginal and incompetent teachers rarely turn into educational versions of that famous movie dance team, Fred Astaire and Ginger Rogers. The dance of the lemons merely sends one principal's problem to another administrator who must then begin the process of observation, evaluation, and remediation all over again.

Ron Collins describes it this way:

> Many districts have a contractual requirement that any unsatisfactory evaluation be started by October. It is neither realistic nor fair for a principal new to the building to make a judgment that quickly. Principals are then stuck with teachers they do not approve of but that they must keep on staff until the next year. Many teachers working in this kind of system see unsatisfactory evaluations in their futures and request transfers to other schools during the summer where they again keep a low profile until the October deadline passes.

Some estimates put the number of marginal teachers in the United States at 2.7 million (Ehrgott, 1992). Why do so many principals tolerate so many ineffective teachers? Because they know that confronting them will be cognitively demanding, emotionally draining, and physically exhausting.

Principals' Roundtable: Dealing With the Lemons

There are numerous reasons why principals think twice before dealing with a lemon. This roundtable discussion focuses on the roadblocks typically encountered in the course of dealing with what I euphemistically term *instructionally challenged teachers* (ICTs)— teachers who are unable to teach so that students can learn. The participants have collectively served more than 100 years in principalships at all levels (both private and public), from New England to the Pacific Northwest and from the Southwest to the Midwest. Some are seasoned and others are relatively new, but their responses are remarkably consistent—dealing with poor teachers remains one of the toughest tasks of the principalship.

Elaine: What do you feel is the biggest challenge of dealing with ineffective teachers—those individuals whose efforts in the classroom don't get results?

Mary Kay Gallagher: Time is the biggest factor from my perspective. It takes an incredible investment of time to work with an ineffective teacher, and it's time away from school improvement efforts, students, parents, and other teachers. If you devote too much time to low-performing staff members and don't maintain a priority focus on building a professional learning community, the impact of the poor teachers is magnified.

Doug Pierson: I'm also frustrated about the amount of time and effort that is necessary to resolve the issues that arise from these types of teachers. To do this work well is very time consuming, and it has to be done consistently. That pulls a principal away from other things that also need to be done.

Carol Kottwitz: Time is definitely an issue with me, too. So many tasks are required of administrators that it's difficult to meet with a teacher regularly. I need support from central office to reduce the amount of paperwork they require to allow me to focus on the needs of teachers. Of course, this is a pipe dream and the real challenge of being an effective leader.

Cathie West: I currently supervise a staff of seventy-four certified and classified staff members. Keeping track of everyone's performance and progress and then providing needed interventions is a huge challenge. I often work seventy hours a week.

C. J. Huff: Follow-through is a challenge for me. As the building leader, I'm pulled in hundreds of different directions. When I have an ICT to deal with on top of all of my other responsibilities, finding the time and energy is difficult.

Todd Lambert: I am lucky to have great teachers, and I work in a building with very few discipline problems, but there are so many other problems competing for my time. We have 620 kids, and the pressure for their success ultimately falls on me. I have a lot of irons in the fire and persistent follow-up is hard. I realized this year that I was spending about eighty percent of my time on about ten percent of the teachers. The biggest problem is that they take away from my time to get into the classrooms to clearly understand the instructional practices of our staff as a whole. In turn, this lessens my ability to provide meaningful professional development based on the needs of the staff.

Elaine: What else stands in the way of dealing effectively with teachers who can't teach?

Cathie West: For me, the negotiated contract and the union are huge roadblocks. The negotiated language surrounding the whole employee supervision and evaluation process is designed, in my opinion, to intimidate principals, protect the incompetent, create jobs for union personnel, and beef up the income of school law attorneys.

Corinne Archie-Edwards: When major problems have occurred, the interference is from a contract and union perspective. While central office support may eventually come, the contract is typically so binding that nothing can be done except to start a long, tedious process of paperwork and waiting.

Shirley Johnson: Contract factors are Number 1. Because too much of what we say as principals can be interpreted as threatening in teachers' opinions, sometimes I pick my battles. I sometimes make concessions, just as my teachers do. There is an informal power source in my building as well, and I work to please her a lot, in order to "calm the rest of the natives."

Carol Kottwitz: I agree. When the union gets involved, it is almost impossible to resolve a situation, so I try at all costs to work slowly through the process so that the teachers do not contact the union. If they do contact the union, it has been my experience that lack of support from central office will force me to back down.

Doug Pierson: I have actually found that I can use the union contract to my advantage as long as everything is on the up and up. Telling a teacher and union representative exactly what the issue is and what needs to be done to correct it should be able to be done in the context of the contract.

Elaine: What about the toll that the whole process takes on your level of stress?

Doug Pierson: I put a teacher on an improvement plan nine years ago, was immediately slapped with a harassment charge, which then turned into sexual harassment and then sexual assault. It has just been settled now, after nine years. At the end of this year, I suspended a staff member without pay, after going step by step through a progressive discipline plan, only to be slapped again with a harassment charge.

Elaine: Being involved in multiple lawsuits could definitely make one think twice before tangling with difficult teachers.

Doug Pierson: Fear of what might happen or the unpleasantness of doing this work is always a factor, but it should never prevent a principal from doing what is right.

Lydia Zuidema: In terms of stress, there are days when an issue has consumed my mind and heart more than it should. During these times, I am more prone to illness, and it's hard to leave school at school.

Carol Kottwitz: Ineffective teachers succeed in making everything take longer than necessary to accomplish. This just plain wears a person out!

C. J. Huff: When you know that even the smallest issue might result in an inflammation of teachers' feelings of inadequacy, it is hard to find the courage and energy to deal with them. Nobody understands what you are going through. and the rest of the building only gets one side of the story—the one they hear in the teacher's workroom. Quite honestly, ineffective teachers suck you dry physically and emotionally.

Elaine: We talked earlier about unions and the impact they have on your ability to deal effectively with ineffective teachers. What role does central office play in this process?

Gwen Watson: The biggest factor that interferes with my dealing with ineffective teachers is a superintendent who is afraid the union will be upset if he doesn't side with the teachers. He was hired because of union pressure on the school board and consequently he's always trying to smooth out any volatile issues that pertain to the union's membership. So it all comes back to the union.

Doug Pierson: At times, a principal feels unsupported by central office administrators, and that is a terrible place to be when doing this very difficult work, but it still must be done.

Elaine: What happens to the dynamic in your school when you start dealing seriously and directly with incompetent teachers?

Doug Pierson: No matter what size the school is, everyone knows everything that is going on, especially in a case of trying to improve a teacher. Sometimes a staff can be divided in its loyalty to a staff member and knowing what is the right thing to be done for the school community. Everybody in the community wants things to be better but not everybody knows the best way to achieve that goal.

Elaine: In the face of obstacles such as these, dealing with ICTs demands strong instructional leadership and a commitment to the mission of the school.

CHARACTERISTICS OF INSTRUCTIONALLY CHALLENGED TEACHERS

Three factors make it imperative for you to deal with ICTs in timely ways: (1) ICTs adversely affect the ability of students to learn, which in turn impacts their test scores, the quality of their effort and work, discipline referrals, and parent and student complaints;

(2) they contaminate the culture of your school and inhibit school improvement efforts; and (3) they jeopardize your effectiveness as an instructional leader.

ICTs fall into three basic categories, as indicated in the chapter title: (1) teachers who are *confused* either about specific aspects of instruction or about their roles as teachers, (2) *marginal* teachers who have significant deficiencies in one or more areas of instructional expertise, and (3) *incompetent* teachers who just plain can't teach and are beyond remediation. Many teachers in these three categories also happen to be angry, troubled, and exhausted—physical and emotional states that further compound their abysmal teaching performances. ICTs with multiple issues are a high priority.

Confused Teachers

Confused teachers fall into two categories: (1) *novices* who have just graduated from teacher-training programs and either need time to mature and fine-tune their teaching or should have been washed out during student teaching and (2) more *mature teachers* who at some point along their career paths have become confused about their roles.

Q & A

Cliff: How can I prevent my new and probationary teachers from becoming angry, troubled, exhausted, or confused? I'd like to ensure that they avoid the professional traps into which many of their senior colleagues have fallen.

Elaine: Get to them before the union does. Let your new hires know that you do their evaluations and hand out the perks. Build professional relationships with them. If you hired them, they should have a strong sense of loyalty to you. Hook up new teachers with your most positive staff members. The union in my district always provided a buddy for every new teacher, but that buddy's foremost goal, all propaganda to the contrary, was to nurture strong union membership. Make sure that your orientation session includes a little infomercial regarding the importance of cultivating a relationship with you.

Confused Novices

Most novice teachers are like apprentices in any field—they need time to mature and acquire the tools of their craft. Most new hires fit in right away and, given encouragement and mentoring, become highly effective teachers. However, every now and then, an exceptionally confused graduate slips through the interviewing process by saying all the right things.

The ink on Sandra's certificate was scarcely dry when she joined my faculty as a long-term substitute for an upper-grade teacher going on a maternity leave. The departing teacher was one of my finest, and she provided detailed plans, an introduction to a teacher buddy who was knowledgeable, and her telephone number in case Sandra had any questions. That was precisely the problem, however. Sandra *never* asked any questions. Without consulting anyone, she decided to reorganize everything in the classroom from the ground up, including rearranging the furniture, changing the class rules, throwing out the lesson plans and grade book, and bringing in her own curriculum. As you can imagine, "her" class of sixth graders did not take kindly to a stranger taking over "their" classroom where the culture was strong and structured. Panic set in and pandemonium prevailed.

> **Principals would be heroes and heroines, not only to students, but also to teachers, parents and the community if they ensured that all teachers were passionate about all students' academic and social achievement.**
>
> **—Former Principal Margaret Garcia-Dugan**

I remember one of several conferences I held with Sandra in an attempt to rescue her from impending disaster. We were talking about the number of complaints from parents and students as well as the mounting discipline referrals from her. She blithely reassured me, "I'm not losing any sleep over this yet."

I stared at her in disbelief. "Well," I said, in my most administrative voice, "I'm glad you're not losing any sleep, Sandra. But the problem is, I am." I had already spent hours doing damage control for Sandra, and she never did get it. To restore a modicum of order in the classroom for the last month of the school year, I was forced to hire a substitute for my substitute. Sandra was too confused to continue.

Confused Veterans

The second category of confused teachers is made up of veteran teachers, many of whom could be outstanding but for the fact that they hold erroneous views regarding the purpose of education, schools, and teachers. Principal Cathie West refers to the teachers in this group as *coasters* because of their desire to coast when the going gets tough. Here's the mental picture she paints with this term: A team of hard-working teachers is pulling a massive wagon loaded with at-risk and difficult-to-teach students— English language learners, special education students, and those who qualify for free or reduced lunch. The coasters are walking alongside the wagon, refusing to pull their share of the load. They insist on teaching only the top group.

Another principal calls the teachers in this group "spoiled." He describes them as teachers who have primarily taught in well-to-do neighborhood schools where all of the students succeed in spite of their teachers. Spoiled teachers are unwilling to go the extra mile for the rising number of at-risk students who are moving into their schools. They expect students to come to school ready to learn and if they aren't, it's not their problem.

I have my own label for this fast-growing group of individuals— Lake Wobegon teachers (LWTs). LWTs think they live in that fictitious Minnesota town, Lake Wobegon, described by humorist Garrison Keillor (1985), as the place where all the children are above average. LWTs believe that they were specifically called to teach above-average students, knowing with smug certainty that they are above-average teachers. LWTs exhibit several other characteristics as well. They refuse to deal with issues of school improvement, accountability, and professional growth. After all, if LWTs and their students are already above average, there should be no need for improvement. LWTs want to coast through teaching with as little effort as possible, an easy thing to do when students already know most of what they are expected to learn. LWTs prefer student-initiated, creative, serendipitous lessons characterized by clever activities, discovery learning, global themes, and most of all, fun. They abhor achievement, outcomes, standardized tests, and data and refuse to discuss ways to raise student achievement in their grade-level teams. Their students already achieve! LWTs are just spoiled enough to think that they get to choose what, when, and whom to teach.

LWTs are trapped in the past and are either unwilling or unable to embrace the new paradigm that demands improvement, accountability, and constant professional growth. In the new paradigm, teaching is no longer a "nice" job with periodic extended vacations, short hours, and great benefits. It has become a bottom-line enterprise demanding that teachers use research-based materials and methods to get results. Focus your assertive interventions with these confused teachers on disaggregated data, the mission of your school, and their job descriptions.

Marginal Teachers

"A marginal teacher is borderline between competent and incompetent. The marginal teacher may do enough just to get by for an evaluation but then slip back into a chronic pattern of poor teaching" (Lawrence, Vachon, Leake, & Leake, 2001, p. 2). There are tens of thousands of marginal teachers (MTs) who hang on to their jobs for one or more of the following reasons: (1) They have excellent social skills and are pleasant people, (2) their principals and their schools are dysfunctional and low performing, or (3) they work in low-paying, small, or rural districts where teachers are in short supply.

There is both bad news and good news regarding MTs. The bad news is that their students are unable to achieve to their full potential—especially students at risk of failure. The good news is that marginal teachers *are* able to learn new methodologies and improve their instruction *if* confronted with their inadequacies and offered assistance and support from a strong instructional leader. Marginal teachers *can* improve *if* they are motivated and cooperative and *if* you provide professional development that is focused, intense, explicit, and very direct. They benefit from collaborative efforts, peer coaching, and willingness to accept assistance from others.

Incompetent Teachers

In contrast to marginal teachers who have just a few instructional weaknesses, incompetent teachers have multiple and serious problems in every area of instruction and management. They are a headache for principals, an embarrassment to their colleagues, a detriment to their students, and a worry for parents. There are at least three conditions that mandate the immediate move of a teacher from the marginal category to incompetent:

1. If MTs are defensive, argumentative, and uncooperative, they are incompetent.

2. If MTs are unable to improve even after intense professional development and multiple types of assistance, they are incompetent.

3. If MTs generate an overwhelming number of complaints from students, parents, and colleagues, they are incompetent.

Case Study: The Incompetent Teacher

Most articles and books regarding how to deal with incompetent teachers tend to focus solely on procedural and legal issues. They often give the impression that the identification and remediation or dismissal of instructionally challenged teachers is nothing more than checklists and timelines. Our case study, a condensed diary written by a novice principal, gives you a glimpse of the emotional and psychological consequences of a first-year encounter with an incompetent teacher.

June 7

I signed the contract for my first administrative position. I am ecstatic! I will be the principal of Walton School, a K–6 building with about 375 students in a small working-class community.

August 29

My first day begins with a stress management workshop in the morning, followed by faculty meetings in the afternoon.

September 22

I am beginning to get a feel for the teaching styles of the faculty. Many are outstanding, but Grace Stevens, an upper-grade teacher, concerns me. Something happens nearly every day that makes me wonder about her understanding of building rules and regulations. I document these incidents and mention them informally to Grace. She seems unconcerned, even surprised, that I should care.

September 29

Although I have been in and out of Grace's classroom quite a few times, I have not made a full-length, formal observation until today. I am highly agitated during the observation of a forty-minute math lesson. In discussing a recent test, she refers to problems that have been missed and to the students' poor performance. Half the class is trying to figure out what Grace is talking about, since she has not returned the test papers. The rest of the students are talking to each other.

October 20

I am disturbed about Grace's continuing lack of attention to schoolwide procedures, but what concerns me the most is the kind of teaching I see going on in her classroom. I speak to my superintendent, Dr. Martin, and he suggests that I prepare a letter detailing the various incidents and give it to Grace.

October 25

I meet with Dr. Martin and the attorney, Bill Peterson. Bill is knowledgeable about teacher dismissal and he shares information about an ongoing case. He encourages me to document, document, document.

October 31

I receive a full-page rebuttal from Grace to my letter of October 20th. She states that my requests for compliance with school rules and procedures are unreasonable and that she has always tried to "do the right thing."

November 11

Five new members are seated on the school board. Dr. Martin suggests that we inform the new board of my concerns about Grace Stevens, and I meet with them and the superintendent in a closed session. Board members want to know if Grace has received poor evaluations in the past. The board president mentions that she has taught for thirteen years, that her previous evaluations have been satisfactory, and that her former principal is still in the district. I am uneasy with the direction the questioning is taking. Dr. Martin handles the discussion skillfully and I breathe more easily.

November 21

I arrive at school to find that the front of the building has been spray painted. There are many obscene references to Grace. I spend most of the day questioning students and find that two boys from Grace's room are the culprits. The boys have never been in trouble before, according to former teachers, and are top students. All the boys would say is that they were angry at Grace. I suspend them from school for three days.

December 21

I am grateful for a few days of respite from worrying about what Grace will do next. Dr. Martin acts very supportive and keeps telling me to write everything down and confer with the teacher, but he doesn't seem to realize that talking to Grace doesn't work.

January 3

The new year has begun. I visit Grace's room around 9:15 a.m. and students are "doing their own thing." It's prime teaching time and Grace doesn't even try to get their attention.

January 6

Three students from Grace's room report to the gym teacher that she has been grabbing and hitting them. After school, I call the superintendent and tell him that Grace is reportedly physically abusing her students. Dr. Martin says he will call the attorney. I leave for the weekend drained from the frustrations of the week.

January 10

The superintendent calls to tell me that Grace Stevens phoned him at home last night to discuss the letter she received from me. I am angry but also relieved. Finally, there is a response from Grace about the problems that have been swirling about her. I receive another parent complaint regarding Grace's physical abuse of a student.

January 13

Dr. Martin and I hold a conference with Grace. We discuss the necessity of complying with district rules and procedures and of refraining from physical punishments. Grace denies ever being physical with students. Later, I observe her classroom again. Students and teacher are in two different worlds.

January 23

I communicate with the superintendent in writing about my frustrations. I need help desperately! I suggest a number of possibilities, such as reassigning some students to other classes, employing a half-time aide, reassigning Grace to another school, or making a concerted effort to dismiss her immediately. Dr. Martin and I meet later in the day, and he directs me to inform Grace "in no uncertain terms" that what is happening in her classroom is unacceptable. He tells me to ask Grace to paraphrase for me what I have said in order to make sure she understands. I leave the meeting with a profound sense of discouragement. I know at this point that talking to Grace accomplishes nothing. But the system demands that I keep on doing it. I exercise great self-discipline and am always professional. I am calm and in control. I would like nothing better than to see Grace walk into her classroom and be an effective teacher, but deep down I know it will never happen, and I resent playing games. I am committed, however, to doing everything in the most professional way. I observe, document, discuss, document, confer, document. I am creating an enormous paper trail.

January 31

I talk to Dr. Martin once again. Since school resumed in January, I have had 12 different meetings with parents, students, Grace Stevens, the psychologist, the social worker, and the superintendent regarding the deteriorating situation in Grace's classroom.

February 2

I have an extended conference with Grace to address her lack of communication with students and parents, her instructional practices that result in students being off task and inattentive, and the use of physical punishments in her class. Talking with Grace is one of the most frustrating experiences I have ever had. Her response is either disinterest or denial.

February 9

Grace Stevens responds to a letter I have written by telling me that all the other teachers in the school should be required to do what I have asked of her. I continue to make observations and document them. I continue to receive complaints from parents and students regarding practices in her classroom. Grace seems powerless to control her classroom. She says that if she had a different group of students she would be much better able to handle the situation.

February 17

I observe Grace's classroom once again. It requires a great deal of professional self-discipline to keep from sending her to the office and taking over the class. Students simply pay no attention while Grace is teaching. They talk quietly with each other, get up from their seats and leave the room at will, or read library books.

February 20

I give Grace a copy of her formal evaluation. The form rates a teacher's performance in fifteen different areas, and I rate Grace unacceptable in every one. I provide extensive comments and documentation to support my ratings.

February 22

The union's regional representative, Rick Johnson, calls me. Grace has been to see him and is concerned about her evaluation. He wants to see me tomorrow.

February 23

I meet with Rick Johnson. He conferred with Grace for over two hours. He says, "We have a problem, and I'd like to do what I can to assist with it." As our conference continues, I have the feeling that Rick doesn't know what to do with Grace, either.

February 24

It is Friday and the end of a very long week. Grace and I meet after school in my office. We discuss her evaluation. She presents me with a letter written in very formal language that says she needs further documentation to support the statements I have made in her evaluation. It appears to me that Grace had some legal help in writing her letter.

February 28

I talk with the lawyer about my conference with Grace. He advises me to continue to observe Grace's class regularly. In addition, he says I should observe her class being taught by others—in art, music, and gym. He suggests having a second individual, such as the district curriculum coordinator or psychologist, make a formal classroom observation. He instructs me to draft a response letter to Grace's letter insisting that she correct the problems identified in the evaluation.

March 1

Grace and the union's grievance chairperson, who teaches in the building, approach me before school. They are filing a grievance about my formal evaluation. I call Bill Peterson, and he advises me that I must state to Grace and the union rep that my professional observation stands as written. Another student reports physical punishment. His story is confirmed by other students. I speak to Grace and once again remind her that physical punishment is not appropriate and is prohibited by board policies. She denies the boy's story. I call Dr. Martin to inform him of this latest development. He advises me to call Bill Peterson again.

March 9

Two more students report physical harassment from Grace. I call Dr. Martin to let him know that Grace's problem seems to be escalating. He tells me that the problem has now moved from the building level to the district level, "from your office to mine."

March 12

I deliver still another letter to Grace, reminding her in very strong language that she is in violation of school board policy. One copy goes in her file and one to the superintendent.

March 19

Grace is absent, and I receive a note from her doctor indicating that she is under medical care and will not be returning to her teaching duties until April 2. Her substitute is a fantastic person. She has stepped into a horrendous situation and nearly turned it around. Discipline, teaching, and learning have all returned to Room 6. I enjoy walking past the classroom and eavesdropping.

March 29

I make a presentation to a closed session of the board of education. Bill Peterson is there. He and the union representative have been negotiating a financial settlement in exchange for Grace's resignation. The school board unanimously supports this arrangement.

April 2

Another teacher is hired to replace Grace Stevens. There are rumors that I harassed her out of the building. Others feel that "she just had a bad class." Most of the faculty members are grateful that their good teaching is no longer considered comparable with what Grace was doing in her classroom. I am comforted in knowing that I have done the job I was hired to do—provide the best possible climate where students can learn.

HOW TO DEAL WITH
INSTRUCTIONALLY CHALLENGED TEACHERS

If teachers exhibit inappropriate behaviors that are directly related to their instructional responsibilities, regardless of where they fall on the competence and experience continuums, conduct AIs. If they recognize and agree with your descriptions of their inappropriate behaviors, make statements to you regarding their willingness to change these behaviors, and subsequently show demonstrable evidence of improvement, continue to use AIs to keep them on track.

If teachers are hostile and aggressive, unwilling to respond even after several attempts to engage them in discussion, and incapable of carrying out simple directives or making incremental changes in behavior and attitudes, AIs are undoubtedly too little and too late. Your approach at that point will depend on their level of teaching competence and whether they are tenured.

Confused Novices

At the first indication of a problem with confused novices, whether instructional, procedural, or attitudinal, conduct AIs. Exhibit 6.1 is a sample AI conducted by a principal with Sharon, a new first-grade teacher. Just one week into the school year, she is oblivious to the mandated schedule. Dr. Moxon doesn't delay in confronting Sharon with her inappropriate behavior. Looking the other way when teachers exhibit any kind of inappropriate behavior, even if it seems minor, sends the message that you don't care. The experienced teachers on the first-grade team are aware of what Sharon is doing and may even have confronted her about it. They are now watching to see how the principal responds.

Dr. Moxon's AI with Sharon contains his sixty-second presentation of the problem (Stage 1 as described in Chapter 2). The story continues when Sharon responds to his request for an explanation with a contrite apology for her oversight and assures him that she was confused about the schedule, believing it to be just a suggestion, not a mandate. She further tells him that she will never make this mistake again. He carefully monitors the situation and is distressed to see that Sharon is still exhibiting inappropriate behavior. In addition to taking extra recesses at odd times of the day, she is also leaving school five to ten minutes early each day. At this point, Dr. Moxon asks himself the following questions:

1. *Is Sharon's confusion regarding the daily schedule a more deep-seated problem?* Temporary problems are amenable to direct instruction and coaching. Teachers with personality disorders usually fall apart under the slightest pressures from students, parents, or the principal. It appears that Sharon's problems need close watching. Even though it is early in the year, Dr. Moxon has questions about Sharon's attitude and understanding of her role as a teacher.

Exhibit 6.1   Assertive Intervention: Sharon

Name: Sharon   Date: September 15

Prompt	Principal's Statement
Behavior to be eliminated	Sharon, I want to talk with you about something I noticed yesterday for the first time. You took your students out for recess three times.
Explicit description of the behavior	According to the daily schedule for first grade that you received in orientation and we then reviewed in our opening faculty meeting, recess for first-grade students is scheduled only once per day and must be taken at the scheduled time with other first-grade classes in order to ensure appropriate safety and supervision of students.
Principal's feelings about the behavior	I'm concerned that after being made aware of the schedule on two separate occasions, you chose to ignore it. We are committed as a faculty to raising student achievement, and utilizing time wisely is an essential aspect of reaching that goal.
Explanation of how the behavior impacts the teacher	Ignoring rules as you have this week is a serious matter that reflects on your professionalism and sends an unfortunate message to your colleagues. I hope you are aware that failure to follow rules could result in your not being rehired.
Principal's personal contribution to the continuance of the behavior	If our presentation and discussion of the daily schedule was unclear to you or if you got the impression from what I said that you had a choice in the matter, I apologize. But let there be no mistake right now. You are required to follow the rules and regulations established in the district.
Principal's desire to resolve the issue	Now that I've clarified this matter with you, I want to be assured that you will begin following the rules immediately, and to make sure that you stay on track, I'll continue to provide support and supervision.
Principal's invitation to the teacher to respond	Tell me what's going on here from your perspective, Sharon.

2. *Is Sharon able to reflect on her performance?* If novice teachers cannot respond and react appropriately during Stage 2 of an AI, prospects for a turnaround in performance are unlikely. Sharon apologized for her behavior and promised that it would not happen again, but it appears that either her response was insincere and manipulative or she has another problem. If Dr. Moxon offers a second-year contract to Sharon and she fails to change during her second year, he will need to be prepared to provide the documentation to deny tenure to Sharon.

Be prepared for the aftermath that can follow the release of a popular or politically connected untenured teacher. Some faculty members, central office administrators, or school board members may perceive you as arbitrary, but your goal is to hire and retain only the best, brightest, and most effective teachers.

Confused Veterans: Lake Wobegon Teachers

AIs are ideal tools to use with LWTs. Their problems are usually based on attitude and commitment difficulties. LWTs are a huge impediment to school improvement efforts because they are not pulling their weight. Helping them rise above their anger or frustration about the shifting paradigms in education can, if successful, give them a renewed vision for why they became teachers in the first place. Exhibit 6.2 is a sample AI with an LWT. Bob teaches math at the high school level and refuses to pay attention to the students in his class who are struggling. He routinely assumes that all students have the prerequisite knowledge and skills to be successful in his classes and when they aren't, blames them (or their parents or former teachers) for their failure.

Bob responded positively to the presentation shown in Exhibit 6.2. He prided himself on being a professional and was deeply disappointed by his lack of success with low-performing students. He took the challenge offered by his principal to visit the classroom of a teacher in a cross-town high school whose at-risk students routinely achieved high grades on AP tests in mathematics. The

Exhibit 6.2   Assertive Intervention: Bob

Name: Bob   Date: September 2

Prompt	Principal's Statement
Behavior to be eliminated	Bob, I want to talk with you about how your attitude toward at-risk students is affecting their achievement in your classroom. You constantly make negative statements about these students and their parents during discussions in team and faculty meetings.
Explicit description of the behavior	Let me show you what I mean. (Now is the time to bring out the disaggregated data showing the low achievement of minority and at-risk students in the teacher's classroom.)
Principal's feelings about the behavior	I'm upset that up to now you've seemed unconcerned and even uncaring about what the data I've shown you means—not only in terms of the mission of the school, but more importantly, in the lives of the students in your classroom. I'm distressed that you haven't taken ownership and responsibility for the achievement of all of your students, not just those who are above average.
Explanation of how the behavior impacts the teacher	You once had an excellent reputation as a teacher, but as I look at the data, it's telling me that you are only effective with certain groups of students.
Principal's personal contribution to the continuance of the behavior	I should have had this conversation with you quite some time ago, but I hoped that you might figure out on your own that your negative attitudes about school improvement were holding you, your students, and the whole school back. I'm sorry I didn't step up sooner to offer my assistance.
Principal's desire to resolve the issue	I want to resolve this issue today. I'd like to know that in the future, our discussions will focus on how we can work together to make sure all of your students achieve.
Principal's invitation to the teacher to respond	I want to understand what's going on here from your perspective, Bob. Talk to me about this issue.

following year was one of Bob's best. All of his students were achieving, and the state mathematics association recognized him for his success.

Marginal and Incompetent Teachers

To deal fairly and effectively with both marginal and incompetent teachers, you need a thorough understanding of what an effective teacher looks like, as well as a complete toolkit of methodologies and resources. If you aren't an instructional virtuoso and budding staff developer, the process can be intimidating. And to further discourage your efforts, there are many "experts" who insist that teaching defies definition:

- "Teaching is a dynamic, evolving activity that cannot be neatly packaged or succinctly defined . . . [often] characterized by mess and noise, by people—lots of people—by caring and heartache, and most of all, by uncertainty and vagueness" (Goodwin, 1987, p. 30).
- "There is no such thing as a behavioral definition of teaching and there never can be. We can never simply watch a person in action and be sure that something called teaching is going on" (Jackson, 1968, p. 77).
- "Teaching is impossible. If we simply add together all that is expected of a typical teacher and take note of the circumstances under which those activities are to be carried out, the sum makes greater demands than any individual can possibly fulfill. Yet, teachers *teach*" (Lee Shulman as quoted in Perkins, 1992).

Given the foregoing statements, it is tempting to back off from instructionally ineffective teachers—intimidated by how much you don't know, rather than being motivated by how much the ineffective teachers can't do. Yet look around your building. The majority of teachers *are teaching*. They are doing it superbly, and nothing less should be expected or accepted from everyone else.

You *do* recognize incompetence the minute you walk into a class-room for the first time. You also see evidence of it in the observational, survey, and assessment data you have gathered: (1) formal and informal assessments of students from a given teacher's classroom, (2) parent and student complaints about the teacher, (3) observation notes collected from dozens of hours of personal observations in classrooms, and (4) data from classroom assessments, such as the praise-criticism ratio of the teacher or the students' time on task.

If you need assistance with providing support for incompetent teachers, there are many books describing the competencies of effective teachers (e.g., McEwan, 2002b), other volumes that outline the supervision and evaluation process, helpful titles on planning professional development and building learning, and still others that will lead you step by step through the legalities and procedures of teacher evaluation, remediation, and dismissal.

Models built on concepts like supportive supervision, collaborative conversations, and reflective inquiry will only work with mature, effective, reflective, and professional individuals who have a desire and ability to change. Collaborative or indirect models don't work with marginal and incompetent teachers. Marginal teachers need close supervision and direct instruction about what constitutes effective teaching. Many marginal teachers have the potential to become more effective, but only if they maintain a positive attitude and are willing to work very hard. Some marginal teachers have never received the benefits of solid instruction and modeling in their teacher-training programs; some have never worked in settings with high expectations or a strong professional development emphasis, and some chose to be teachers for all the wrong reasons and are simply trying to hang on for the pension. Marginal teachers are a drag on school improvement initiatives because their students do not achieve at the levels of which they are capable.

> **To say that you have taught when students haven't learned is to say that you have sold when people haven't bought.**
>
> —*Madeline Hunter, in a 1989 workshop*

One discouraging characteristic of MTs is that even though they are unable to keep their teaching at a high level for any consistent period of time (for whatever the reason), they always know just when to notch up their performance to make you *think* they are finally improving. This slight improvement usually occurs during your summative evaluation observation. Then, when you relax—they relax! And, when they relax for the third or fourth time, be ready to declare them incompetent to teach students in your school.

Q & A

Elaine: What kinds of strategies do you typically use to help MTs improve their instruction?

Cathie West: My first goal is always to lead teachers to explore the problem, identify underlying causes, and generate ideas for improvement. These discussions typically take place in the third phase of an AI (the motivational phase).

Elaine: What do you think is the biggest roadblock when it comes to improving instruction?

Cathie West: Not being explicit enough about exactly what is going wrong in terms of instruction. I always explain in detail what a teacher is doing *right* and doing *wrong* with many, many vivid examples.

Elaine: Then what do you do?

Cathie West: I visit the teacher's classroom frequently to check on progress, reinforce successes, and give corrective feedback. Just one visit doesn't do it. You have to be in the classroom of a marginal teacher two to three times a week. I also find another teacher who will serve as a mentor and then provide release time for the marginal teacher to visit the mentor's classroom as well as for them to consult together.

Elaine:	At what point do you make the decision to move a teacher from the marginal to the incompetent category?
Cathie West:	If you have nurtured a confused or marginal teacher for a considerable length of time (two years is tops for me) but are still getting nowhere, it's time to let the teacher *know* in no uncertain terms that things are *still* seriously wrong. At this point, I involve a union representative and create a formal improvement plan. I have found that raising teachers' anxiety levels works when nothing else seems to make a difference.

Beware of MTs who tell you confidentially that they are planning to retire at the end of the year. This is a favorite ploy to relieve the intense pressure you are putting on them. If you back off, these individuals often feel relieved and decide to stay another year. By that time, you have lost months and must begin the process once again. Until you have MTs' resignations in hand, they must remain on your radar screen. Gather data and document marginal teachers as carefully, persistently, and often as you can. Don't rely solely on formally scheduled observations. Many MTs have one good lesson they pull out every year for their evaluation observation, and if you only get one chance, you may be forced to give this teacher a satisfactory rating—simply because the lesson they taught *was* satisfactory.

Engage in frequent walk-throughs that focus on critical variables of effective instruction. Effective teachers are effective all day, every day. That is the message you must send to the marginal teacher who talks a good game but simply can't or won't deliver on a consistent basis. Conduct AIs to confront the brutal facts—if teachers only teach well once in a while, they are not effective teachers.

There are three possible scenarios that can occur as you deal with marginal teachers: (1) They improve dramatically and with consistent coaching and supervision are able to maintain a satisfactory performance; (2) they improve slightly and need more intense help, but you have other priorities and they slip off your radar screen; or (3) they move into the incompetent category. Lawrence and his colleagues (2001) suggest that you satisfy four prerequisites before making a recommendation for termination:

> Prerequisite 1: You have established administrative and instructional credibility with the staff.

> Prerequisite 2: You have effectively monitored the instructional climate in all classrooms, and you have provided assistance to those teachers who are having difficulties.

> Prerequisite 3: You know the physical and psychological demands inherent in the dismissal process. (The additional time and energy required to document a marginal teacher's deficiencies are immense; therefore, you must be committed to following through with the process.)

> Prerequisite 4: You have discussed the process with individuals in central administration as well as the attorney for the school district to obtain their support and to ensure that legal and contractual obligations are met (p. xii).

We have already determined that AIs are not appropriate tools for use with incompetent teachers. In the absence of guidelines from your central office and legal counsel regarding how best to document teacher incompetence, I recommend FRISK®, a documentation model developed by attorney Steven Andelson in cooperation with the Association of California School Administrators and the California School Boards Association. [Note: To obtain a FRISK® book or to inquire about training in the model, contact Atkinson, Andelson, Loya, Ruud, & Romo in Cerritos, California, at 562-653-3453.] The letters in the acronym FRISK® stand for

> (1) facts (What did the employee do?), (2) rule (What should the employee have done?), (3) impact (What was the impact or possible impact of the employee's conduct on the district?), (4) suggestions-directives (When and what do you want the employee to do to improve performance in the future? What

will happen if there is no improvement? How can you help the employee improve?), and (5) knowledge (Does the employee have knowledge of personnel file rights and applicable labor contract provisions?).

Questions reprinted from
Andelson, 2001. (Used by permission.)

The FRISK® Documentation Model helps you to put everything in writing in a format that satisfies legal requirements in the event of a teacher dismissal. When you are developing documentation for a possible dismissal, everything of significance *must* be put in writing that is explicit *and* legally defensible.

SUMMING UP

These are the "big ideas" regarding how to deal with confused, marginal, and incompetent teachers:

- Know yourself. Dealing with incompetent teachers requires stamina, organizational skills, knowledge, and the ability to withstand being accused and abused by teachers, union representatives, and occasionally even the individuals who are supposed to be on *your* side.
- Know the pitfalls. Dealing with incompetent teachers is a legal procedure. Much of what you will have to do is tiresome, repetitive, and often seems illogical. Don't argue. Just do it.
- Know the commitment that is required. Don't start unless you intend to stick with it.
- Know the experts. Get help from central office. If at the outset, your superintendent or other central office staff don't seem too excited about what you want to do, keep phoning, writing memos, providing evidence, and calling meetings. Eventually they will get the idea that you know what you are doing, you are right in what you are doing, and you are not going to go away.

- Know your legal counsel. You will of course have to be introduced by the superintendent since every minute you spend or talk with a lawyer on the phone will be billed to the district. Read all you can. Use the FRISK model.
- Get organized for the long haul. Find a way to get your paperwork and files in order. Thank goodness for computers and copy machines. I dealt with ineffective teachers without technology. But I did it.
- Be persistent and consistent.

Sixty Ways to Affirm, Energize, and Empower Teachers

Before you start this final chapter . . .

Think about how much affirmation is going around your school.

Appreciation, praise. Unfiltered, unqualified. There is so little of it going around.

—Scott (2002, p. 193)

I t's very stressful to work for someone who doesn't believe in praise and affirmation. One of my former bosses had the misguided notion that handing out a positive word would somehow diminish my incentive to work or give me the idea that he was a soft touch. He believed that positive feedback was negative and negative feedback was positive. I *know* what bosses like these say when they are questioned about their stingy attitudes—"If my employees are doing a good job, they know it." These miserly masters think that if they give affirmation and encouragement on the job, their employees will suddenly become complacent and take the boss for granted. These modern Scrooges are fearful that productivity will plunge if people are satisfied in their work. They might do well to read Dickens's *A Christmas Carol* again, all the way to the end.

Organizational theorist Douglas McGregor (1960) called this management approach *Theory X*—the belief that employees exist for the benefit of the organization and need to be directed and corrected, not nurtured and needed. *Theory Y*, on the other hand, postulated that people will be more productive if the environment takes into account their social, emotional, and self-actualization needs (Hersey & Blanchard, 1977, p. 55).

Just ahead are sixty ways to put Theory Y into practice: affirm, energize, and empower your teachers. Some of the suggestions are easy to implement, while others may require a paradigm shift. Skim through the items until you find an idea that captures your attention. You can't implement them all, but consider where your faculty might need re-energizing and do at least one thing differently tomorrow.

1. Don't Play Gotcha

If I were to return to the principalship, here is the list of personal expectations I would share with all new hires and frequently review for veterans. You no doubt have your own set of must-dos for new hires. Help people be successful by spelling out your expectations.

- *No surprises.* "I want to be kept informed of any difficulties you encounter with parents. I need to be aware of problems in order to give you the support you need."
- *Apologize.* "I will support you, but only if you apologize for inappropriate behavior and ill-advised decisions (e.g., whacking a student over the head with a rolled-up newspaper, even if it was in fun; going on a spontaneous walking field trip without notifying anyone; or showing an R-rated movie, even if you did fast-forward through the objectionable sections)."

- *No blame.* "I will not tolerate any blaming of parents when kids don't learn or behave. You may feel this way from time to time, but please do not ever speak the following words within the halls and walls of this school: 'If only the parents would . . . ' After my years in education, I have come to believe that if parents *could*, they would. They want to, but they don't know how. They would like to, but they don't feel qualified."

- *Open your door.* "I expect your door to be open to parents at all times and that you will place two adult-sized chairs just inside your door. Parents need not make special appointments to visit your classroom. They just need to stop in the office and make their presence known and then follow the rules that we have jointly established. Please inform me of any parents who abuse this privilege, and I will deal with them immediately and appropriately. Failure to observe the guidelines we have jointly established to govern parent visits will result in the revocation of parents' visitation privileges."

- *Communicate.* "Don't wait until midterm to let parents know of an academic problem. Don't wait for bad news to call a parent. Call first with good news or a positive introductory phone call."

- *Evaluate homework.* "There is no excuse for homework assignments that students are not able to complete independently. Do not send home assignments unless you have already conducted an 'I do it; we do it; you do it; apply it' teaching sequence."

2. Keep It Short but Sweet

Leave short notes of encouragement or affirmation on teachers' desks or in their mailboxes: "Great lesson plans this week" or "I received two positive phone calls from parents about you this week. Stop in to see me and I'll tell you about them." Notice the small things that teachers do so they know you are paying close attention to their instruction.

3. A Calling Card

Order professional-looking business cards for teachers with the school logo and the title *Educator* underneath their names.

4. The Power of Listening

Encourage informal visits from your staff. The opportunity to just talk for a few minutes to a principal who can provide some Wordless Advice can be uplifting to a discouraged teacher. If you are not familiar with Wordless Advice, look up the entry *Advise* in the A section of the Communicator's Handbook.

5. One Goal at a Time

Choose one major focus for the school year and work together as a staff to address it. When you have reached the goal, solidify what you have accomplished and continue to move ahead with a new goal. This gradual approach to change makes each year feel increasingly productive and eliminates the stress and burnout that is inevitable if you never finish anything.

6. What Do You Think?

Ask teachers, either individually or collectively, for their advice regarding specific problems. Use this technique for situations in which you do not have answers or predetermined plans and genuinely need teacher input. Staff members get cynical if you ask for input with no intention of taking their advice.

7. The Healing Touch

Hire a massage therapist to set up a chair in the teachers' lounge and offer complimentary massages during the lunch hour or after school. Not every staff member will participate, but for those who appreciate a healing touch, the gesture will be remembered for a long time. In a study of sixty school children who had been traumatized by Hurricane Andrew, researchers at University of Miami's Touch Research Institute found that depression dropped in kids who received thirty minutes of massage twice a week for a month, whereas kids who watched a relaxing video showed no improvement (Kalb, 2003). Massage will calm stressed teachers as well.

8. I Appreciate You For . . .

Think about each of your staff members individually (even the difficult ones who keep you awake at night). Select one quality, attitude, or behavior of each teacher that contributes to a positive culture in your school and write a short note of appreciation. For example, "Thank you for the empathy you show to the parents of difficult students. You always seem to know just what to say." Or "Thank you for the way in which you can foresee possible problems and road blocks in a plan we are developing and point them out in helpful ways. This quality helps us avoid glitches in our implementation of new programs." If you have teachers whose behavior fails to support your positive school culture in any demonstrable way, invite them into your office for AIs.

9. A Gift From the Lincoln Leopard (or Your School Mascot)

Teachers never seem to have enough money in their supply budgets to purchase the extras they want (e.g., books for a classroom library, materials for a unique science experiment, or posters to decorate their walls). When my teachers began to find $50.00 money orders in their mailboxes from the Lincoln Leopard (our school mascot), they were overjoyed. The "anonymous" gifts appeared in just two or three mailboxes per week. They were obviously coming from an "insider," but they were never able to determine who was behind this random act of kindness. The PTA treasurer assured me that no one was drawing funds from *their* checking account. The mystery of who was doing it and which staff members would receive their gifts next became a hot topic of conversation. The Lincoln Leopard Caper, as it came to be known, energized teachers. It also reminded them that the best gifts are those that are given with no expectation of public recognition.

10. Trading Spaces

Trade places for a period or two during one day per week with selected teachers to show your appreciation for something they have done that went beyond their job descriptions. They will "be" the principal and you will "be" the teacher.

11. Random Acts of Kindness

In the spirit of the Lincoln Leopard Caper described earlier, engage in random acts of kindness for your faculty members. For example, order pizzas to be delivered anonymously to the staff lunch room during the noon hour. Purchase a small bouquet of fresh flowers for a teacher who has had a tough week and leave them anonymously in the classroom. Send an anonymous cheer-up card to someone who is going through tough times.

12. Time Is Money

Administrators often bemoan the contract stipulations regarding the length and frequency of meetings. But in some instances, we have only ourselves to blame since we frequently fail to voluntarily respect the worth of teachers' time. Make sure that all of your meetings begin and end promptly. Use the allocated time wisely and agree on ways to expedite administrivia, such as producing a daily or weekly bulletin that keeps everyone informed of meetings and deadlines.

13. Test Your Teachers' Empowerment Index

Short and Rinehart (1992) have developed a School Participant Empowerment Scale that assesses the level of teacher empowerment within a school community. If you are looking for an action research project or are concerned that your teachers feel helpless and out of control, use this scale to gather data prior to developing an action plan.

14. Release Me

Hire substitutes so that teachers at various grade levels or departments can be released from their classrooms to work as teams on issues of concern: (1) evaluating progress of their at-risk students, (2) setting team goals for an upcoming month, or (3) fine-tuning a lesson to teach a critical learning outcome.

15. No Surprises, Please

There's nothing like a last-minute change in the schedule to upset even the most angelic teachers. I'll never forget a Friday inservice I presented to a group of high school teachers whose weekly routine had been disrupted by two evenings of parent-teacher conferences sprung on them at the last minute by the central office administration. The hostility in the cafeteria was so thick you could cut it with a knife. No wonder the principal disappeared to his office after he introduced me. Respect your teachers' schedules and private lives by planning ahead and sticking to predetermined timelines.

16. Put Together a Winning Team

"Coming together is a beginning, staying together is progress, and working together is success." (Henry Ford)

In cooperative learning circles, the stages of a group coming together are called forming, storming, norming, and performing. Too often, teachers are solitary souls, closing their doors to work with their students. To give them the skills and knowledge they need to be effective leaders or team members, offer team-building training for your entire faculty or for a leadership team within the faculty. Do it yourself if you can, or find someone in a nearby district or from your regional service center to give training in problem-solving techniques, group process, and communication. My favorite book of team-building exercises is *100 Ways to Build Teams* (Scearce, 1992).

17. Empower Your Staff Members

"Empowerment begins with the belief that all people are capable of taking action to improve their work. The process gets underway when leaders express faith that others can and will meet high expectations." (Bellon, 1988, pp. 30-31)

Empowered teachers are in charge of their own destinies. They have control, input, responsibility, and a sense of efficacy (i.e., confidence in their own ability to teach all students and make a difference in the classroom). Their personal sense of worth and self-respect keeps them motivated and energized in their classrooms and in their relationships with colleagues.

Principal Bill Lamperes (2004) identified ten strategies that enabled his high school staff members to take responsibility for decision making and ownership of the day-to-day operations of the building. He describes the strategies in a helpful article in *Principal Leadership* that can be retrieved online: http://www.principals.org/publications/pl/pl_10_strategies_0204.cfm

18. Teacher Appreciation Award

Many schools give out monthly or yearly awards to grade-level teams or classrooms that demonstrate school spirit or good citizenship. Come up with an award for groups of students that find ways to appreciate their teachers and treat them respectfully. Nominations for the award can come from the teachers themselves, if they feel their class deserves the award, or from parents or administrators who have observed students treating their teachers in exemplary ways.

19. Attend Special Events

Middle and high school administrators know the importance of showing up for concerts, athletic competitions, and dramatic presentations. To make sure that your presence does not go unnoticed, write a thank-you note to the coach, conductor, or director that mentions something particularly outstanding about the event. At the elementary level, encourage teachers to invite you to special events or interesting lessons in their classrooms and then make absolutely sure you get there on time and stay for the grand finale. Write a thank-you note to the class afterwards, complimenting both them and their teacher on their outstanding performances.

20. Eliminate Distractors and Time Wasters

Don't mandate silly procedures that waste teachers' time and demean their professionalism. I can think of one example in particular that even now irritates me. In one building where I taught, teachers were expected to collect their staplers, pointers, flags, plan books, curriculum guides, and teachers' manuals at the end of each school year, cart them all to the office, and wait in line at the secretary's desk to check in before they were given their final paycheck. It was a demeaning and time-wasting exercise.

21. Management by Wandering Around

Don't underestimate the importance of wandering around (informal classroom visits and walk-throughs). In a study of how the strategies, behaviors, attitudes, and goals of principals impacted teachers' classroom instruction, Blase and Blase (1998) found that "wandering around enhanced teachers' motivation, self-esteem, sense of security, and morale" (p. 109). Furthermore, MBWA, as management by walking around is sometimes called, was also strongly linked to the reinforcement of existing good teaching behaviors. A more recent incarnation of MWBA is focused on leading staff to reflective inquiry (Downey, Steffy, English, Frase, & Poston, 2004).

22. Respect the Lesson

Never interrupt teachers when they are directly teaching students. Don't engage teachers in lengthy discussions during walk-throughs, even if they are not directly teaching students. Interruptions like these are distracting to students as well as teachers. Don't permit specialists, parents, other teachers, or instructional aides to interrupt teachers while they are teaching. Do not permit intercom announcements during the teaching day. Don't cancel classes for impromptu assemblies or programs. In Japan, the lesson is sacred. Make it so in your school.

23. Be a Good Sport

If you live in an area where college or professional sports are a part of everyday life, use sports as a motivational tool. When the Chicago Bears were in the Super Bowl, I was principal of a school in the area, and we challenged another school to a Math Facts Super Bowl. When the Cubs were doing well (I think that happened once during my tenure as a principal), we wore T-shirts and hats to support them. A first-grade teacher had gone to high school with an NFL quarterback who, whenever he was in the area, visited our campus to motivate the kids and captivate the teachers.

24. Tell It Like It Is

Level with your teachers. They know when you say one thing and think something else. Take Susan Scott's (2002) advice: "Begin to overhear yourself avoiding the topic, changing the subject, holding back, telling little lies (and big ones), being uninteresting even to yourself" (p. 11). Scott goes on to say, "Most people want to hear the truth, even if it is unpalatable" (p. 18). If you can model telling the truth in love, soon your teachers will be able to say what they are really thinking. The culture and climate of your school will change dramatically.

25. Pass It On

Pass on every positive comment you hear about your teachers directly to them. If appropriate, do it at a faculty meeting. If not, share it with the teacher privately. Better yet, put it in writing for the teacher's personnel file.

26. Set Sensible Goals

Set meaningful, measurable, and attainable goals. There is nothing more demoralizing to a teacher then a list of ten meaningless and unattainable goals. Accomplishing one goal well is cause for celebration.

27. Solve Big Problems Together; Solve Little Problems on Your Own

The way some principals approach problem solving reminds me of the man who told a friend that he and his wife had divided the decision-making duties at their house in a very equitable fashion. "I make the big decisions and she's in charge of the little stuff," he explained.

His friend pressed him for examples. "Well," he said, "I decide when to invade Afghanistan and she decides which stocks to buy and sell." Just make sure that you and your teachers agree on what decisions are important and which ones are insignificant.

28. Be a Resource Provider

To work together effectively in small groups, teachers need resources and training. Provide (1) funds for materials, (2) release time during working hours for planning sessions, and (3) training in how to work in teams.

29. Plan for Change

You may be the kind of leader who is eager for challenges and can quickly change direction and focus. Respect the reality that some of your faculty members are not as eager to take risks and reverse directions as you may be. Here are some guidelines to help you plan ahead for change:

- Do the groundwork necessary to ensure smooth change well in advance. Prepare a list of the proposed changes, stating the advantages and disadvantages, and give it to the teachers early in your planning.
- Try to think of all the objections they might possibly raise and answer them before they are asked.
- Bring all of the members of your team together and go through your written list, pointing out both the positive and negative aspects of each change. In this way, you will gain their trust as they realize that you are not trying to put one over on them. Ask for feedback and listen actively to whatever they have to say. Tweak the plan using their suggestions.
- Take teachers' fears seriously and do what you can to set their minds at ease. Should they raise objections, make sure that these are specific and detailed rather than general indications of disapproval. This will help them think about what they are saying and their attitude in general.
- Find a way to overcome each objection, if possible. If you cannot, describe to them any positive benefits and try in this way to win their support. Remember that, even after changes have been made, it will take time for them to accept them fully, so it may be necessary for you to keep an eye on the situation for a while (Markham, 1993, p. 133).

30. Teach

"There is no better way to become personally involved in the nitty-gritty of the teacher-student experience than by teaching." (DuFour & Eaker, 1987, p. 92)

DuFour and Eaker (1987) point out the benefits of principals returning to the classroom regularly to teach: (1) a closer relationship with students, (2) greater empathy for teachers, and (3) greater credibility with teachers.

31. What's Important?

Communicate your expectations to teachers explicitly and directly. Leave nothing to chance or guesswork. Fuzzy expectations result when *you* haven't identified *what's important.* I enjoy using an enchanting picture book by Margaret Wise Brown (1949), *The Important Book,* to illustrate the concept of *important.* Read it aloud at a faculty meeting, choose several problem areas that need discussion, and ask your faculty to write their own page in the picture book. For example, if communicating and getting along with parents has become an issue, the question becomes, *What's important about parents?* Your teachers can no doubt generate a list of statements about parents, such as: (1) Parents are the biological or adoptive guardians of their children, (2) parents are responsible for bringing up their children and keeping them safe, (3) parents believe their children can do no wrong, and (4) parents want the best for their children. Once the list of statements has been generated, the task becomes identifying the "*important* statement" about parents (in the style of Brown's book). For example: *The important thing about parents is that they want the best for their children.*

32. Celebrate Small Successes

Don't wait for end-of-the year test scores to celebrate. If one child achieves a milestone, celebrate it. If one group moves on to the next level, have a party. If a grade-level team reaches a difficult goal together, put up a banner in the teachers' workroom

33. Take the Blame

If an initiative fails, take the blame. If an initiative succeeds, give the credit to your teachers.

34. Cooperate

"Few teams develop to their full effectiveness without a good deal of nurturing and conscious development." (Francis Ana Young, quoted in Jones & McBride, 1990, p. 7)

Cooperative learning is a very effective instructional methodology. Structure staff development, faculty meetings, and grade-level meetings so that teachers will have opportunities to experience for themselves the power of sharing and learning with others. Not only will their classrooms be enriched, but your school will also become a more cooperative place. Form interschool teacher teams, carefully selecting members for balance in various areas of strength and need. Provide resources and incentives for the various teams to get results with students, produce lessons and curricular materials, or solve difficult problems in the school (Johnson & Johnson, 1989, p. 73). Often, the best teachers will freeze out the ineffective teachers, so make it worthwhile for better teachers to mentor, support, and work with their less effective peers.

35. We Did It!

Use the word "we" exclusively when talking about the accomplishments of your school.

36. What's in a Name?

"What's in a name? That which we call a rose by any other name would smell as sweet." (William Shakespeare)

Although Romeo and Juliet were able to fall in love and sustain their relationship even after they discovered they bore the names of rival families, their laid-back approach to surnames is not the norm. Teachers care deeply about their names. Make sure that every teacher who uses a classroom has a nameplate outside the door. When a third-grade teacher earned her doctorate, I had a new nameplate mounted outside her door immediately. Purchase professional-looking name badges for people to wear when they go to meetings outside of your school. Make sure that you can pronounce and spell the names of each of your faculty members correctly. Display a staff directory in the front hallway. Romeo and Juliet may not have cared about their names, but your teachers do!

37. Feed Your Faculty

Serve food at faculty and professional development meetings. There's nothing more discouraging to me than to present a workshop for teachers where there are no creature comforts, such as food, beverages, workshop supplies, name tags, and comfortable adult-sized chairs and tables.

38. Serve Your Faculty

Cook breakfast (or lunch) for your faculty once a year. If you don't (or can't) cook, have it catered or make reservations someplace special.

39. Enough to Go Around

Purchase enough materials for everyone to have their own personal copy. Don't expect teachers or students to share important materials they use every day.

40. Be a Role Model

Attend every inservice you expect teachers to attend. Sit up front, participate, do the exercises, and answer the questions. Don't whisper asides, talk on your cell phone, leave the meeting to attend to an imagined emergency, reorganize your daily planner, or read your mail. All of these behaviors send the message that either you are too important for staff development or that staff development is not important to you.

41. Support New Programs

Whenever a new curriculum or program is implemented, go to the training sessions and then teach lessons at various grade levels. Only if you experience the curriculum firsthand will you be able to coach and support your teachers. Budget money for coaches, release time, and additional training sessions for those teachers who may need extra help during implementation.

42. The Open-Door Policy

Leave the door to your office open. Smile and wave to people as they go by. Always make time for teachers unless an important scheduled appointment takes precedence. Whenever a teacher walks into your office, stop what you are doing immediately. Smile, stand up, walk over to the round table, and sit down with the teacher. If the inevitable question, "You're not busy, are you?" is asked, reply with, "How can I help you?" Then be ready to do what needs to be done. Whether you drive across town to buy a replacement pencil sharpener for a first-grade teacher, share a teacher's frustration regarding a parent problem, or locate an article that a teacher needs for an evening class, know that you have made yourself available to meet the needs of your teachers.

43. Ready to Work

Make sure that support teachers (media specialists, music, art, physical education specialists, and special educators) are ready to offer their services to students and teachers on the first day of school. Everyone has to be ready to work on the first day—not just classroom teachers. There is nothing more irritating to classroom teachers than to have a specialist of any kind tell them, "We're still getting organized" or "I'm still doing paperwork."

44. A Penny for Your Thoughts

Ask your staff how you are doing at least once a year using the following questions:

- What am I currently doing that is helpful to you and supportive of your instructional effectiveness?
- What am I doing that is interfering with your effectiveness and should be eliminated?
- Is there anything I am not doing that I should be doing to help you be a more effective teacher?

Use the results to set personal goals and then set about changing unproductive behaviors.

45. Honor the Heroes and Heroines

Honor *every* teacher who retires with an assembly, gift, pageant, letters, poems, songs—even those who gave you sleepless nights. When you honor one teacher, you are honoring all of your teachers.

46. Thirty-Minute, Thirty-Day Rapid Results Goals

If you've ever started a new diet and gotten rapid results, you know how motivating a quick weight loss can be. You can help teachers get rapid results from their instructional efforts by instituting a Rapid Results goal-setting process. The process, in a nutshell, involves a grade-level team holding a thirty-minute meeting to agree on a goal (that must be measurable) for student learning to extend over a one-month period. They agree on how the goal will be measured and what activities will take place. (For more details, forms to use for goal-setting meetings, and the experiences of one principal who used this approach to turn her school around, see McEwan 2002a, pp. 115–116, 168–169.) For a thorough discussion of a results-focused approach to turning your school in the direction you want to go, see Schmoker (1999, 2001).

47. Lend a Helping Hand

Be visible every day. Be especially visible and helpful in those classrooms where angry, troubled, exhausted, and confused teachers are teaching or in areas where large numbers of students are gathered (e.g., cafeteria, playground, or auditorium).

48. Support Your Teachers

Develop a consistent and fair response to handling students who are sent from their classrooms to the office for behavioral infractions. If necessary, collaborate with your teachers to develop a plan that works and is respected and followed by the teachers. There is nothing more demoralizing to a teacher than to send students to the office only to have them reappear seconds later with a smile.

49. Establish a Tradition

Establish a yearly tradition—one that expresses your personality *and* uses your gifts and talent. For example, give ornaments you've made to staff members at Christmas, write a letter during the Thanksgiving holiday detailing the characteristics of your faculty for which you are thankful, purchase a book for everyone that is important to you, or write a yearly Valentine's poem if poetry is your gift.

50. Touching Base

Take time to greet or interact with all teachers each day to let them know that you care. Take whatever time is needed to make sure that each staff member feels needed and appreciated.

51. Discover (and Appreciate) Their Strengths

Help staff members understand and appreciate their differences as strengths that can make the school community more effective. Use a book like *Now Discover Your Strengths* (Buckingham & Coffman, 2001) to help staff members identify their own personal strengths. Or use Edward DeBono's (1999) *Six Thinking Hats* to help staff members appreciate their colleagues' diverse thinking styles.

52. Accentuate the Positive

For every corrective or negative comment you give to a teacher, sincerely offer three positive, affirming, or supportive comments. Take care, however, to deliver positive and negative comments at different times. If you add positive comments to your AIs, teachers may remember only the compliments.

53. Friends

During the past twenty-five years, the Gallup organization has conducted several major research studies among managers and employees regarding the characteristics of effective managers as well as the specific working conditions that improve employee productivity (Buckingham & Coffman, 1999, 2001). Many of these characteristics and conditions have to do with the quality of relationships in the workplace. I have reworded some of the Gallup survey questions to make them more germane to school settings. When staff members can answer *yes* to these questions, their productivity, motivation, and loyalty will be high, according to Gallup's research (Buckingham & Coffman, 1999).

- In the past seven days, have teachers and other staff members received recognition or praise from the principal for effective instruction, their caring attitudes toward students, or special attention and service to parents?
- Does the principal give evidence of caring personally about staff members as people?
- Does the principal encourage and facilitate the personal and professional development of staff members?
- Do the opinions of all staff members count when important decisions are made?
- Does the mission of the school make staff members feel as though their work is important?

- Does every staff member have a best friend at school?
- Do staff members have opportunities to learn and grow through the work they do? (p. 28).

54. Be a Resource Provider

When teachers need things, deliver. If a teacher needs extra handouts at the last minute, duplicate the materials yourself. If a team needs release time to complete a project, find substitutes. If a difficult parent is harassing a teacher, facilitate a solution.

"Resources are anything the principal can use to satisfy teacher needs: materials, student discipline, insulating teachers from parents, organizational maintenance." (Achilles, Keedy, & High, 1999, p. 39)

55. Increase Student Achievement
Through Staff Development

Bruce Joyce and Beverly Showers (1980) wrote a book titled *Student Achievement Through Staff Development*, and the concept has taken on a new direction through the work of Murphy and Lick (2001). The centerpiece is the creation of whole-faculty study groups that wrestle with issues that are key to student learning. For example, a study group might tackle the issue of how best to teach students how to write summaries because data demonstrates that students are having difficulty demonstrating proficiency. The group then acts on the students' needs by generating a list of tasks and activities that need to be completed (e.g., designing a rubric for assessing the quality of a summary; examining the summaries that students generated during the past month; and investigating strategies for teaching students how to summarize using the content areas).

56. Praise

Give specific and meaningful praise. For example, "Your explanation of that statistics formula along with the real-world examples you provided made me understand that subject in a way I never have before. You lesson was the essence of clarity."

57. Troubleshoot

Solve problems as quickly as you can. Solve simple and uncontroversial problems on your own. Deciding whether to order scented or unscented toilet tissue for the faculty bathroom doesn't require a task force. However, if the problem is a pervasive instructional problem, such as the number of students who are failing to achieve eighty-five words correct per minute fluency by the end of second grade, a task force of primary teachers will be needed to investigate.

58. Deliver on Your Promises

Do what you promise to do. Don't make promises you can't keep. Promise less than you plan to deliver.

59. Time Off for Good Behavior

Give people time off for good behavior. If your fourth-grade team has just finished a particularly grueling quarter and accomplished great things, find a way to release them from their responsibilities so they can finish putting grades on their students' report cards. Possibilities for finding such time might include combining classes for PE and offering to teach alongside the PE teacher or combining the class and teaching them yourself. Give your teachers the gift of time, occasionally.

60. Learn a New Trick

Read a book like *First Break All the Rules: What the World's Greatest Managers Do Differently* (Buckingham & Coffman, 1999). Then, choose three practices described in the book and implement them in your school.

Conclusion

As you wind up your reading . . .

Check out the bottom line as summed up by a practitioner:

The bottom line is kids. All children should be able to come to school every day and be greeted by a caring teacher with high expectations. As the building leader, I have the responsibility to make that happen. Sometimes that doesn't come easily. Our goal is always to improve, not remove teachers. Regardless of this outcome, when the dust settles and the smoke clears, it is a huge intrinsic reward to see better instruction and improved student performance. You can see the results of your efforts in the faces of the children.

—C. J. Huff

THE "BIG IDEAS" OF THIS BOOK

As I was putting the finishing touches on this book, I received an e-mail from a principal with a problem:

> I've got an angry teacher who is directing her discontent to (mostly) her fellow staff. This is her third year. She was reassigned a different grade to teach this year. Her anger seems to have been developing since last spring when I informed her of the change and extended a contract. Things came to a head this week.

The principal attached a letter she had written to the teacher after meeting with her, for my comment. The opening paragraph said this: *"First, I want to share with you my support for you as a teacher at Clearbrook Elementary School. I deeply appreciate your service to the students at our school. You have made very positive contributions both in and out of the classroom during your two-plus years here. Thank you for the many hours you spend preparing for your students. I hope I conveyed in our meeting that I consider you to be a gifted and skilled teacher, with much to offer our students."*

The closing paragraph said this: *"Finally, I want to commend you for great progress made in turning in lesson plans and other paperwork on time so far this year. I can see you have made this a priority, and this professionalism shows."*

In between the opening and closing paragraphs, there was one vague reference to the teacher's *"inappropriate verbal and nonverbal body language."*

If you have been a principal, you have likely written similar letters. I know that I have. Because you are a caring and empathetic educator, you are reluctant to tell the plain, unvarnished truth without giving it the "Mary Poppins" touch—a spoonful of sugar to make the medicine go down more readily. You feel that you must say something nice if you say anything at all. This advice, given to you continually by your mother, doesn't work when dealing with tough teachers. All you are doing is making it more difficult for yourself later when a teacher doesn't improve or needs further disciplinary action. Angry, troubled, exhausted, or just plain confused teachers won't get the message if you deliver it along with a gift-wrapped box of chocolates.

As you reflect on the teachers on your staff who need AIs, keep the following "big ideas" in mind:

- Deal with the tough teacher today. Just because you haven't done it so far is no reason to keep on avoiding the problem.
- Deal with the tough teacher directly and truthfully. Don't talk to other people about it. Don't complain to your colleagues and your superintendent. Go to the source of the problem and confront it. Don't pull any punches. Tell it like it is.

- Don't sugarcoat the problem to assuage your guilt or make the medicine go down more easily.
- Deal with the tough teacher systematically. Stop any babbling, and hold the teacher accountable for talking about the inappropriate behavior.
- Deal with the tough teacher quietly and calmly. Don't raise your voice, let your blood pressure skyrocket, or become defensive and accusatory in tone.
- Above all, do it for the children.

Resource A

The Communicator's A–Z Handbook

A

Accept

"On a bad day you don't need a lot of advice. You just need a little empathy and affirmation. You need to feel once again that other people have confidence in you." (Lamott, 1994, p. 157.)

Teachers who are troubled or exhausted need acceptance. If they feel that you aren't interested, don't care, or are prematurely passing judgment on them, they may well get cold feet and leave without telling you about the problem. Teachers need the freedom to explore an issue without criticism or censure. Recall your own days of teaching when a particularly difficult parent or a stubborn student caused you to doubt your expertise. All you needed was someone to affirm and encourage you.

Acknowledge, Agree, Apologize, Appreciate

Highly critical teachers have three missions in life: (1) finding fault with something you have done, (2) pointing out a situation or an individual in the school that needs to be corrected (e.g., the custodian, your secretary, or the new teacher you just hired), and (3) proofreading the faculty bulletin for punctuation errors. I like the advice that Sam Horn (1996) gives in her book, *Tongue Fu!* She suggests taking the A Train to deal with hypercritical people.

Perhaps mention of the A train stirs memories of your first subway ride in New York City, or, if you're fond of big band music, you might think immediately of Duke Ellington's classic. But for dealing with picky people, Horn suggests a different kind of A train, one that takes you and a highly critical teacher to a more productive relationship. Choose one or more of these four possibilities: (1) acknowledge, (2) agree, (3) apologize, or (4) appreciate. Here's how the A train works. *Acknowledge* the existence of the problem to the critical teacher, if indeed the problem is a real one. *Agree* that it is a worthy problem that needs a solution, if indeed it does. Don't be reluctant to *apologize* (either personally or corporately) for what did or didn't happen (if appropriate). And if you are feeling particularly magnanimous, express your *appreciation* to the teacher for bringing the problem to your attention, indicating that you will do all in your power to correct it.

Don't become defensive or accusatory. Of course, taking the A train only works when picky teachers identify real problems that *can* be solved. Teachers who complain about things over which neither you nor they have any control (e.g., the number of students who don't speak English, NCLB, and the changing demographics of your school) have a different set of problems. They are either angry (see Chapter 3), exhausted (see Chapter 5), or confused about their roles as educators (see Chapter 6 for a discussion of "Lake Wobegon" teachers).

Advise (wordlessly)

You may well have all of the answers, but don't give them to teachers whose sole purpose in visiting your office is to talk. It has taken me years of practice to perfect the art of giving what I call *wordless advice*, not only with teachers who are upset but with my own family members. I finally learned that when people come to me with a problem, they don't necessarily want advice; they just want an empathetic ear. They don't want my eyes to glaze over and my mind to drift to personal agendas; they want my full attention and thoughtful nods and "hmms." They don't want me to talk "at" them, either. They need a sounding board, a place to reason out their own problems. By the time they finish their monologues, they thank me for the great advice (I never said a word) and go merrily on their ways.

Assert

Lack of self-differentiation will impact your ability to handle difficult teachers. (See the discussion of this topic in Chapter 1 for more information). On the other hand, if you feel confident and worthwhile, you will be able to put the words and deeds of angry teachers in perspective. Remember, angry teachers are like dogs and horses. They sense when you are unsure or hesitant and will take over before you know it.

Here in Arizona where I live, mountain lions are not uncommon. A leaflet distributed by the National Park Service advises hikers and campers to do the following if they meet a mountain lion: "Always give them a way to escape. Don't run. Stay calm. Hold your ground, or back away slowly. Face the lion and stand upright. Do all you can to appear larger. Grab a stick. Raise your arms. If you have small children with you, pick them up. . . . The goal is to convince it that you are not prey and may be dangerous yourself. If attacked, fight back!" (Wildlife Hazards for Campers and Hikers, 2004). These suggestions may seem somewhat humorous or even outrageous when applied to angry teachers, but there are some lessons to be learned here. Be confident. Don't let angry teachers back you into a corner or scare you. Stand tall and do all you can to appear in charge, in control, and willing to stand your ground.

Attend

"If I have ever made any valuable discoveries, it has been owing more to patient attention, than to any other talent." (Sir Isaac Newton)

Attending means giving people your undivided interest. This skill is important for all interpersonal communication, but it is absolutely essential when dealing with troubled or exhausted teachers. Attending means using your body, face, and especially eyes to say, "Nothing exists right now for me except you. Every ounce of my energy and being is focused on you."

This kind of intense concentration calls for structuring one-on-one time with teachers in an atmosphere that is free from interruptions. Clear away clutter. Remove anything that might interfere with your focus. Turn off the telephones and shut the door. Do nothing but *attend.*

B

Backtrack

Backtracking is a form of feedback in which you repeat back *some* of the same words or phrases that another person is using (Brinkman & Kirschner, 1994, p. 45). Although paraphrasing (different from backtracking) is often recommended as a way of confirming that you have understood what someone is saying, perceptive people often resent having their words replaced by your words. To them, that implies that you are twisting the meaning of what they've said. In backtracking, you don't echo everything that is said but instead, focus on key words that capture the main idea. This will let teachers know that you have heard and understood.

Bless

"Almighty, I ask that _____ be blessed with growing self-confidence and the recognition that it is not necessary to put others down to feel good." (Rosen, 1998, p. 197)

Many religious traditions exhort their believers to exercise love, care, respect, humility, and patience in relationships with difficult people. Such encounters are to be accepted as opportunities to learn and grow along one's faith journey, rather than as heavy burdens to bear. I have long engaged in the habit of uttering quick, silent prayers when I encounter people on the highway, in the supermarket, or in a social group whose behavior I find to be inappropriate. My prayers do not petition for miraculous changes in these difficult individuals; that would be presumptuous and arrogant. I only ask that God would bless them at that moment. I never know how God has answered my "flash prayers," but I do know that my attitude of blessing creates more understanding, patience, and empathy on my part.

Psychologist Mark Rosen (1998) also advances the idea of offering silent blessings for those individuals who are oblivious to the effects that their critical, hostile, and demeaning attitudes and words have on others. A sample blessing is shown in the foregoing epigram. Others can be found in his helpful book, *Thank You for Being Such a Pain: Spiritual Guidance for Dealing with Difficult People.*

Bracket

An important part of true listening is a mental exercise called *bracketing*, the temporary giving up or setting aside of one's own assumptions and prejudices to experience as far as possible the speaker's world from the inside (Peck, 1978, p. 73). The natural thing to do to when difficult teachers walk through your door is to retrieve and replay all of the unpleasant conversations you've had with them. But in order to bracket, you must set aside bad memories and embrace their world anew.

Breathe

"One of the best ways to release tension is through breathing." (Crowe, 1999, p. 226)

When confronted with angry teachers, there is a tendency to stop or slow down your breathing. It's almost as if momentarily suspending this natural bodily function will keep the clock from moving ahead and stop difficult teachers in their tracks. The kind of shallow breathing that moves only your chest and shoulders is stressful and adds to your feelings of tension and stress. Deep breathing (through the diaphragm muscle in your lower abdomen) lowers your blood pressure, relaxes your muscles, and slows your heart and respiration rates. In fact, deep breathing actually reduces anxiety (Weiss, 2004).

C

Confront

Although I defined the term *confront* in the Preface, I repeat the definition here for those readers who may have missed it.

Although the definitions of *confront* and *confrontation* often include the concepts of defiance or antagonism, there is a third meaning that I prefer: *acknowledging and meeting problem teachers face to face with honesty, boldness, and confidence.* To confront teachers in the context of this book means making those individuals aware in a forthright way that you have observed their behavior or heard what they have said, are comfortable about defining it in detail and naming it for what it is, and can discuss it in a calm and rational way. Furthermore, you are willing to lend support and resources if needed to address the problem, but you will not ignore further manifestations of the problem. Confrontations as described and used in the context of this book are never arrogant, hostile, or antagonistic. Rather, they are respectful, persistent, and consistent.

D

Demonstrate

Sometimes videotape is worth a thousand words—either to show someone how to do something they are *not* doing or to point out something they *are* doing, the reality of which they cannot accept. Of course, before you tape, get permission. To make the process less threatening, suggest that teachers watch their videotapes alone the first time, to take in what they are doing on the screen. Then, if appropriate, suggest that they view their videos with trusted friends. Last, ask them to view the videos with you. Perhaps pictures will be more effective than the thousands of words you have tried thus far in your attempts to convey a message.

Do (it)

"To change one's life, start immediately, do it flamboyantly, no exceptions." (William James)

Once you have finished reading this book, you will have several options for dealing effectively with angry, troubled, exhausted, and confused teachers. The question is, How do you feel about the fact that you haven't done it so far? I hope you are eager to begin making the seven habits described in Chapter 1 your own.

If you are wondering how to do it *flamboyantly*, as suggested in the epigram, here's my interpretation: Deal with your teachers in such a way that they actually take what you have to say seriously. Don't be subtle. Make a statement. Let me explain. If you're a male, making a statement is the same as wearing a new tie that is totally out of character for you. People notice it immediately. If you're a female, making a statement means being as noticeable as changing your hairstyle or even the color. People can't miss the fact that you changed from a brunette to a redhead overnight. Stop fading into the woodwork when you deal with difficult teachers. Confront them assertively.

E

Empathize

"Seek first to understand, before you seek to be understood." (Covey, 1989, p. 235)

To empathize means to lay aside your own needs to be heard and understood and instead focus on hearing and understanding what teachers have to say. Just remember, however, that with difficult teachers, a little empathy goes a long way. If you engage in too much handholding over a Kleenex box with troubled teachers, you will find yourself in the full-time counseling business with little energy left for important instructional leadership tasks. Your goal when working with difficult teachers is to help them be productive in the light of their difficulties, not to excuse and enable them to withdraw from their teaching responsibilities into full-time counseling in your office.

Enlist (Them)

When nitpicky teachers find a problem in your school that they want you to solve, enlist their help in solving it. Principal C. J. Huff explains:

I had one teacher in particular who was always ready to do battle any time she walked into my office. Once I got to know her a little better, I sensed her insecurities as well as her desire to be respected by her peers. I delegated a small project for her to be in charge of that year. It really made a difference in terms of how she approached me and, more important, how she perceived herself. That relationship has continued to grow but needs a little nurturing from time to time when she slips back into her old ways.

F

Forgive

"If you devote your life to seeking revenge, first dig two graves." (Confucius as quoted by Hallowell, 2004, p. 10).

You may think of forgiveness as a religious concept, and indeed, "forgiving one who has harmed you liberates you from the emotional prison you have created for yourself . . . [and] is a deeply spiritual act" (Rosen, 1998, p. 255). But forgiveness is also an essential way of being if you intend to remain in the principalship for any length of time. You may think of forgiveness as something you do for someone else, but in reality, it is something you do for yourself. To retain the slings and darts of angry teachers in your psyche is a sure way to lose the vision of why you became a principal in the first place.

Cathie West suggests that when you have been attacked, it is like being on center stage with everyone watching to see what you'll do next. If you act in a professional manner, you teach your staff how you want *them* to behave, and you teach the attacker that antagonistic behavior holds no power over you.

G

Give (Resources, Affirmation, and Credit)

Giving is one of the seven habits needed for being able to deal effectively with teachers, whether they're difficult or not. (See

Habit 5, Being a Contributor, in Chapter 1.) In fact, even highly effective teachers can feel resentful when their administrators are stingy with resources, affirmation, and credit for their hard work and creativity.

H

Help

Helping teachers won't garner accolades or win awards for you. But it communicates a deep sense of commitment and caring to those who receive your assistance. Whether washing down tables in the cafeteria, rolling up your sleeves and helping with a last-minute collating session to finish the school newsletter, or just assisting a teacher with a particularly challenging group of students, *helping* sends this message to staff members: "You and your job are so important to the mission of our school that I am willing to put my agenda on hold and pay attention to yours."

I

Intuit

"The most important thing in communication is hearing what isn't said." (Peter Drucker, 2004)

Infer and intuit. Sometimes teachers don't have the courage to say what they need or want to say. If you can decipher their intent and feed it back to them for confirmation, you can ease their concerns without their having to fully articulate them. This is a tricky strategy and must be used with discretion. See the discussion with Jane, an angry teacher, following Exhibit 2.2 (the sample assertive intervention) in Chapter 2. When Jane is unable to articulate what is really on her mind, her principal infers and puts words in Jane's mouth. Jane immediately relaxes knowing that now she won't have to figure out a way to share the truth.

J

Jolly (Them)

"A merry heart does good, like medicine." (Proverbs 17:22)

To jolly someone is to encourage them to be pleasant and cheerful. Laugh every day. Find the humor that abounds in your school and let it tickle your funny bone. Laugh at yourself. It can often help you sail through difficult interpersonal situations. I remember a stressful situation with my superintendent. I thought he was interfering where he didn't belong. He was trying to help me avoid embarrassment. I ignored his advice, thinking I knew better. But I didn't, and I blew it. An apology was in order, but I decided that my superintendent needed a little jollying along with my apology. I stopped at the bakery and bought several pies—lemon meringue, coconut crème, and an apple for those who preferred "healthy" desserts. I set the table before the administrative cabinet meeting with plates, forks, and fancy napkins. As the team members arrived, they glanced at the goodies wondering whose birthday it was. I told them I'd explain when the superintendent arrived. Once we were all assembled, I told them that the pies they saw on the table were prepared using a very special recipe—they were "humble pies." We all laughed, my team members empathized, and the superintendent was appreciative. A potentially explosive situation was diffused, and my apology was a sweet one.

K

Know (Thyself)

"Pity the leader who is caught between unloving critics and uncritical lovers." (Anonymous)

Identify a small group of faculty members whom you trust to provide feedback regarding what's working and what's not, in terms of your leadership. Don't wait for your critics to line up with complaints. Get the straight scoop from people who support you and want you to succeed. Get to know yourself well so you can start working on the parts that aren't done yet. Whenever Cathie West takes a new principalship, she meets with the union representatives right away. She tells them that they have an important job—to keep her, their new principal, out of trouble. She reports that this invariably provokes laughter, but the reps do take her words to heart and keep her informed about leadership snafus and any discontent brewing in the school.

L

Listen

I personally have always had a very hard time listening. Impulsive and easily distracted, my mind has "a mind of its own." It could be wandering elsewhere, outlining a new book or making up a to-do list. I might be thinking of what I want to say in response or formulating the perfect solution to the problem being presented. I've learned the hard way that these approaches don't win friends, influence people, *or* solve problems. Because I am also hearing impaired, I must overcome yet another set of challenges to effective listening. If I lose the main idea, recovering it without appearing inept is almost impossible. Here are my listening rules:

- Do not respond with your own message by evaluating, sympathizing, giving your opinion, offering advice, analyzing, or questioning. If you must talk, simply report back what you heard in the message as well as the attitudes and the feelings that were expressed.
- Make occasional and appropriate verbal responses, such as "oh," "hmm," or "uh-huh," to confirm to the speaker that you are paying attention. Teachers need to feel that you understand them both emotionally (e.g., their feelings of anger or fear) and intellectually (the actual words they are saying).
- Keep listening until there is a sign that the teacher has finished speaking and is ready to listen to you.

- Take notes (if appropriate to the situation) to help you remember critical details of the conversation. Most teachers with problems will be relieved to know that you are really listening to them and care enough to write it down.

Lower (the Boom)

"Lowering the boom" is an expression from the world of sailing. The *boom* is a horizontal attachment to the mast. As the story goes, if the captain of a sailing ship wanted to discipline an unruly crewman, he would lower the boom by dropping it down full and swinging against the wind, thus causing the boom to swing suddenly across the deck. The uncooperative crewman would be swept over the side of the boat. Whether he was plucked from the drink by his crewmates or the captain was dependent on how far he had fallen from favor (Word for Word, 2004). The boom you lower on teachers is reality—the truth with which you have never before confronted them. You can't be discrete and subtle with a difficult teacher or they will leave your office feeling good—they have once again hoodwinked you. And you will leave the meeting feeling frustrated. You have to tell teachers in direct and explicit language what it is that they have been doing that they must stop doing or what it is that they haven't been doing that they must start doing. Give concrete examples. Lower the boom. Let them sputter, cough, and choke for a few seconds before you pull them out of the drink!

M

Mirror

Give support and encouragement to emotionally troubled or exhausted teachers by "be[ing] a clean mirror, [neither] descriptive . . . interpretive or judgmental." (Wegela, 1996, p. 160)

Rather than judging or interpreting what teachers are saying, hold up a mirror so they can see what their inappropriate behavior or unwillingness to seek help may be doing to their students, colleagues, or to themselves.

N

Neutralize

"To change a difficult person, you must first change your-self—your way of thinking about the person and your way of responding to the familiar provocations." (Tavris, 1978, p. 294)

Sometimes your first inclination when cornered by angry teachers is to strike back (e.g., counterattack, defend, explain, justify, or just plain cut off and "divorce" individuals you don't like). Instead, step back and remain neutral. Don't personalize the attack and try to convince teachers of their wrongness and your rightness. Instead, self-neutralize—that is, repeat silently, "This isn't personal. It's not about me" (Crowe, 1999, p. 121). And most of the time, it isn't about you. It's about abuse by previous principals, family problems, insecurities, exhaustion, stress, money worries, and fears of failure. Although these problems and issues are very real to the people you are dealing with, *you* must remain neutral about them. Remaining neutral does not signal a lack of empathy or a dispassionate attitude. It means that you should not feel responsible for or take ownership of angry teachers' feelings and behaviors. If they are angry, upset, and troubled, it's not your fault. (Of course, if you really have blown it, by all means apologize and move on.) Do all you can do to defuse their anger, but then relax and sleep soundly. Don't let teachers' anxiety, frustration, and hostility consume your energies and demoralize your own emotional state.

O

Offer (Options)

Use verbal aikido techniques, similar to those used in martial arts (Crowe, 1999). Aikido practitioners don't stiffen their bodies in resistance when an opponent comes at them. Rather, they move forward and down, taking the wind out of the sails of their opposition and diluting the force and effects of a bodily thrust. Rather than telling teachers what they can't have or what you won't be able to do for them because of your policies and procedures, suggest some possible options that *might* work. Of course, you will need to be quick thinking lest you make promises you can't keep, but experience helps and so does asking for time to explore and examine some possible options. Use phrases like the following to open that option door (p. 173):

Here are some options . . .

What I *can* tell you is . . .

What you *can* do is . . .

Which would you rather have?

Give me some specifics so that I can see how to help you.

Have you tried . . . ?

P

Pause

There is no rule that says every problem needs an immediate solution. Always take time to think; any decision (or upset teacher) will benefit from a twenty-four-hour cooling-off period. Never permit difficult teachers to back you into the "I've got to know what you're going to do now" corner. "The wise [educator] knows how to create baffles and buffers to buy time, to absorb heat, to promote collective wisdom, to insure [sic] a maximum sense of legitimacy for final decisions" (Bailey, 1971, p. 225). Here are some ways to slow down the action:

- During a meeting, pause and say nothing, to give yourself time to gather your thoughts. During a long pause, you can sip your coffee or check your notes.

- Regroup by taking a few minutes to summarize the information or progress made thus far.
- Never commit to or even suggest an action that involves other individuals before checking with them.
- Ask for time to gather more information or to consult with a superior. This sends the message that you are serious about solving the problem and want to make sure you're fully informed.
- When a meeting is headed nowhere (e.g., information is being repeated, tempers are beginning to flare, and nothing is being accomplished), perhaps it's time to schedule a follow-up meeting. Consider including some experts at the next meeting to add additional brainpower to the problem-solving team.

Praise (Carefully)

Praising teachers is a highly recommended personnel policy (Blase & Blase, 1998; Ziglar, 1986). However, when working with teachers who are angry, troubled, exhausted, or confused, praise can sometimes be perceived as threatening (Farson, 1996, p. 64). For example, when you praise someone, you are in reality sitting in judgment on that individual, and they may well feel diminished rather than encouraged.

I have experienced that feeling myself on occasion. I was a principal and had just given a comprehensive report to the board of education on the recommendations of the teacher evaluation committee I had chaired. The newly hired assistant superintendent for instruction (whom I had not met) hurried over during a break to tell me, "That was really an excellent report. Very good work." His comments, although undeniably positive, left me feeling strangely uneasy. After reflecting, I figured it out. He was evaluating me to establish distance and superiority over me.

Another problem that difficult teachers may have with praise is that they are used to getting it Mary Poppins style: "A spoonful of sugar makes the medicine go down." The minute you start praising, most dysfunctional teachers will start anticipating the medicine. Use praise judiciously and in the right context.

Q

Question

"Have the humility to grasp the fact that you do not yet understand enough to have the answers and then ask the questions that will lead to the best possible insights." (Collins, 2001, p. 75)

Learn the power of asking the right questions to uncover all aspects of a problem. Ask all of the usual "who, what, where, and why" questions, but you may also find it helpful to use statements such as "I'm not sure I understand. Help me to see why this is so important to you." Offer alternative ways of thinking in the form of questions such as these: "Might it work this way?" or "What if we tried this approach?" Don't be afraid of asking open-ended questions to which you have no suitable answers. But beware of assuming the role of prosecuting attorney in your questioning mode. Clarification, not conviction, is your ultimate goal. There are a number of positive things that can happen as you question teachers with whom you're meeting (Brinkman & Kirschner, 1994, p. 46):

You will gather higher quality information than what is offered.

You can help teachers become more rational.

You can patiently and supportively demonstrate that you care about what they are saying.

You can slow a situation down long enough to see where it's heading.

You can surface hidden agendas and reveal misinformation without being adversarial.

Sometimes, strange and surprising things can happen if you are able to lay aside your own mental models (or paradigms) and consider alternatives. Mental models are "the images, assumptions, and stories that we carry in our minds of ourselves, other people, institutions, and every aspect of the world. Like a pane of glass framing and subtly distorting our vision, mental models determine what we see" (Senge, Kleiner, Roberts, Ross, & Smith, 1994, p. 235).

Senge (1990) offers a variety of conversational scripts for turning encounters with people who are disagreeable into explorations of alternative perspectives. For example, when faced with an impasse, Senge advises asking questions such as "Are we starting from two very different sets of assumptions here? Where do they come from?" or "It feels like we're getting into an impasse, and I'm afraid we might walk away without any better understanding. Have you got any ideas that will help us clarify our thinking?" (pp. 200–201). The notion that your meetings with distressed teachers might actually turn out to be learning experiences may be a somewhat revolutionary idea to consider, but drop your defenses and give it a try.

Chris Argyris (1986, 1991), the noted organizational theorist, suggests that even the most skilled professionals must often "unlearn" how to protect themselves from being threatened before they can ever become truly effective managers. What Argyris means is that to be truly effective communicators, we must unlearn or relearn the automatic responses our brains and bodies make to a perceived threat, drop our natural defenses that cause us to respond in kind, and disarm upset teachers and others with a calm acceptance and willingness to listen, learn, and even grow.

Quit

"Those who know don't talk. Those who talk don't know. Close your mouth, block off your senses. Blunt your sharpness, untie your knots, soften your glare, settle your dust." (Lao-Tzu, 6th century BCE/1988, p. 56)

"Quitting" in this context doesn't mean giving up. It means shutting up. Once you have conducted an AI as described in Chapter 2, quit talking and wait for the teacher to respond. A quiet, expectant silence is a powerful communication tool.

R

Refuse (to Triangulate)

Dysfunctional teachers often want you to do their homework for them. Let me explain. Dan is upset with the teachers on his team. They left him out of their planning session and are now expecting him to enthusiastically adopt their goals. Rather than going to the members of his team (either together or individually), Dan comes to you and demands that you do something about this. Of course, you know exactly why Dan was left out. Instead of confronting Dan about his negativity whenever the team meets, they "forgot" to tell him about the meeting. However, you know that both Dan and his team members need to talk to each other—not you.

Your first question for Dan should be, "Have you talked to anyone on the team about this?" If his answer is "No," then send him straight to the source of his irritation. Beware of being triangulated—caught between two (or more) people who should be talking to each other but instead, are attempting to put you in charge of their problems. You can only hope that given this golden opportunity to let Dan know that they are tired of his naysaying, his team members won't chicken out and make some phony excuse about his memo getting lost.

Relax

Communication consultant Marjorie Brody (Brody Communications, 2004) warns that your body language can often communicate how stressed you feel to those with whom you are speaking. Here are some tips to make sure that you appear relaxed and in control. The message you may be sending with your nonverbal language is shown in parentheses.

Don't stand with your hands on your hips (condescending and arrogant)

Don't cross your arms (closed-minded and stubborn)

Don't tap your fingers or other objects (impatient)

Don't avoid eye contact (terrified)

Don't stare intently (arrogant and intimidating)

Don't droop your face, wrinkle your brow, or turn down your mouth in a frown (distressed, unhappy, or bored)

Don't fidget in your chair (nervous, impatient, or disinterested)

S

Shock

If you are constantly being browbeaten and bullied by angry teachers, shock them into quieting down with this firm assertion:

"Sally, I can understand why you're distressed. I *would* like to talk with you about the unruly student in your classroom and how his behavior is disrupting your instruction. But first you have to sit down, lower your voice, and stop swearing at me. At ABC School, our code of ethics requires that we treat one another with respect. I want no less from you than you are demanding from your students."

Go on to say, "We're not going to tolerate students being rude to you in your classroom, and I can't tolerate rude behavior from you, either. So please calm down and let's begin all over again."

Administering this kind of shock therapy can remind teachers where they are, with whom they are speaking, and what their real priorities are—teaching and learning (Axelrod & Holtje, 1997, p. 87).

Solve (Problems)

The characteristics of good problem solvers are amazingly similar to the qualities one needs to be a good parent or marriage partner: patience, discipline, creativity, continuous improvement, repetition, honesty, and continuous learning (Lynch & Werner, 1992, p. 160). Problem solving is always a part of quality decision making, but solutions do not come without struggle, frustration, and occasional bouts of chaos and messiness. Every theorist has developed his or her own model of problem solving, but most include some variation of these seven steps as "must-dos:"

1. Gather all the facts and define the problem. Rushing to judgment or stating your opinion about a situation before you have listened to the various sides will often result in solving the wrong problem. Very few educational problems need immediate solutions, and the more information you have at your fingertips, the more likely that a quality solution will present itself. Some possible sources of information include observations, test scores, historical data, and consultations with a variety of specialists. Find someone you trust, and use that individual as a sounding board for thinking out loud. If the problem is a sensitive personnel issue, discuss it only with authorized individuals.

2. Identify some possible reasons for or sources of the problem. Beware of responding too quickly with your own expertise. You may know exactly what is needed, but even if you are absolutely correct in your assessment, the other parties involved in the problem (e.g., superintendent, teacher, union official) will need time to reach the same conclusion.

3. Verify the most likely causes. Sometimes, finding a cause is impossible and a waste of everyone's time. In other situations, determining the cause is a guarantee of a quality solution.

4. Identify several possible solutions. Rare is the problem that has only one solution (even in math), so don't get committed to *your* solution too early in the discussion. Assigning blame is counterproductive and anger evoking. Assume that dysfunctional teachers are doing the very best they can given the circumstances of their lives at the present time.

5. Determine the solution that seems best, and then develop an action plan to implement it.

6. Implement the plan. Make sure you give it enough time to work.

7. Evaluate and fine-tune the plan. Look for concrete evidence of success (e.g., more assignments turned in, fewer unacceptable behaviors, more positive interactions between parent and teacher).

Soothe

"A soft answer turns away wrath, [whereas] a harsh word stirs up anger." (Proverbs 15:1, Revised Standard Version).

Gentleness and artfulness are among the most effective ways of defusing anger while at the same time giving you the opportunity to determine its real source (Taylor & Wilson, 1997, p. 67). Gentleness connotes courtesy, refinement, serenity, civility, and patience. If you have a somewhat aggressive personality, cultivating gentleness may feel like an artifice. But you will be amazed to see how strong "softness" can be. The term *artfulness* suggests cleverness and skill, a talent you must cultivate and practice. I know that being gentle in the face of a teacher gone ballistic doesn't feel normal when you first try it, but keep practicing, even when defending, excusing, and accusing come far more readily to the surface of our feelings and actions.

The tone and quality of your voice are just as important as the words you speak. If you are hurried, hostile, defensive, or distracted, your voice will give you away immediately, and others will judge you to be insincere, even if you are saying all the right things. A soft answer means that you don't contradict, correct, condescend, or disagree with teachers who are already infuriated, even if they are misinformed. Don't be impatient or act harried.

Convey serenity with body language that is calm and receptive. Maintain eye contact, sit quietly without fidgeting, and arrange your hands and arms in a nonthreatening way—uncrossed and relaxed. Don't frown, grimace, sigh, play with your hair, crack your knuckles, tap your fingers, yawn, adjust your clothing, roll your eyes, slouch your body, grit your teeth, chew gum, cross and uncross your legs, move too quickly, look alarmed, or make faces. Nod your head occasionally to indicate you understand the speaker. Remain attentive without appearing tense or threatened.

Step (on Some Toes)

"If you never stepped on anybody's toes, you haven't been for a walk." (Kingsolver, 1995, p. 45)

Stepping on somebody's toes is identical to talking straight (see the next entry), telling the truth in love, having a "fierce conversation" (Scott, 2002), and conducting AIs as described in Chapter 2. The "walk" of which the proverb speaks is your journey to self-differentiation and assertiveness. Take the first step today, but don't trample too hard on those toes.

T

Talk (Straight)

"Truth is a hard apple to catch and it is a hard apple to throw." (Donald Barthelme)

Fellow Corwin author, Robert Ramsey (2003), includes the following Seven Step Code of Communication in his book, *School Leadership from A to Z* (p. 128).

1. Say only what's true.

2. Say what needs to be said.

3. Say what you mean.

4. Say it to the right people.

5. Say it as soon as possible.

6. Say it as simply as possible.

7. Keep on saying it.

Ramsey's communication code is another way of stating these "big ideas" of Chapter 1:

Be a character-builder.

Tell the truth in love.

Do it today.

Be assertive.

Tell (a Story)

One technique to use with teachers who are distressed about the difficult parents or students with whom they work is storytelling. Share experiences you have had as a parent, teacher, or principal in which circumstances and problems similar to the ones they are having were eventually solved through caring, kindness, persistence, and love. Storytelling is a technique that can help teachers benefit from past history without feeling as though you are giving advice or telling them what to do (Shinn, 2004).

U

Underpromise

A classic maxim from the business world is "Underpromise, but overperform" (Axelrod & Holtje, 1997, p. 37). This principle also has applications in your dealings with upset teachers. Promise far less than you think you can deliver. There is always the temptation when faced with exhausted or troubled teachers to offer what you think will be a wonderful solution to their dilemmas (e.g., release time, a classroom aide), but first make sure you have the authorization and the money.

V

Visualize

To visualize means creating a picture in your mind of what a good school looks like—the way you want your school to be at some point in the not-too-distant future. Whenever you are tempted to give up, imagine your school with teachers who are productive and satisfied. Picture the day when your teachers work with each other in collaborative ways. Envision a school culture where all students are learning and achieving.

W

Wonder

Don't forget to ask the following questions periodically:

"I wonder what I'm doing to contribute to this problem?"

"I wonder what I need to change about my behavior to improve our productivity and effectiveness?"

"I wonder if there's anything else I could be doing to be a more effective communicator?"

X

Xerograph

Find a role model or mentor to "copy" or imitate. Knowing what a good one looks like (a principal who has embraced and put into daily practice the seven habits of attitude and action necessary to deal with dysfunctional teachers) will enable you to replicate those habits in your own life. Find a principal of character who can serve as a mirror for you own practice of the principalship. Cathie West shares that when the going gets tough, she visualizes administrators she admires for their professionalism and then imagines how *they* would handle the situations she finds challenging. This exercise keeps her moral compass pointed in the right direction.

If I were returning to the principalship, I would review *The Ten Traits of Highly Effective Principals* (McEwan, 2003) and focus on the leadership behaviors of exemplars such as Lola Malone, Terry Beasley, Tom Paulsen, Cathie Dobberteen, and Dale Skinner.

Y

Yeasay

"Yeasayer: a person who is affirmative, positive, etc. in his attitude toward life." (Guralnik, 1980, p. 1647)

A yeasayer is the opposite of a naysayer. A naysayer is negative and nitpicking. A yeasayer is optimistic, cheerful, hopeful, and buoyant. There will always be disasters and downsides. A yeasayer doesn't let those interfere with the mission.

Z

Zip

"A person filled with gumption doesn't sit around dissipating and stewing about things. He's [she's] at the front of the train of his [her] own awareness, watching to see what's up the track and meeting it when it comes. That's gumption." (Pirsig, 1974, p. 303)

A communicator principal has to have lots of zip, energy, and even gumption to deal creatively and effectively with angry, troubled, exhausted, and confused teachers.

Principal C. J. Huff concedes that "[difficult teachers] wear you out." However, in the best tradition of a principal with zip, he is able to look on the bright side of this communication challenge. "Working with these teachers has helped me improve my problem-solving abilities because they give me so much practice!"

Resource B

The Culture Builder's Toolkit

The Culture Builder's Toolkit contains four assessment instruments and six group process exercises, all of which are designed to assist you in evaluating, creating, and nurturing a positive school culture.

PART 1: ASSESSMENT INSTRUMENTS

Part 1 contains four assessment instruments to evaluate the following:

- Your assertiveness as an administrator
- Your progress toward attaining the ten traits of highly effective principals (McEwan, 2003)
- The overall health of your school culture
- The team-building skills of your faculty

The Assertive Administrator Self-Assessment

Description

The Assertive Administrator Self-Assessment, Form B.1, contains fourteen indicators, each one describing a specific characteristic of the assertive or self-differentiated administrator as described in Habit 1, Chapter 1.

Form B.1 The Assertive Administrator Self-Assessment

	Never	Seldom	Sometimes	Usually	Always
Indicator 1	1	2	3	4	5

I protect and honor my own rights as an individual and also protect the rights of others.

	Never	Seldom	Sometimes	Usually	Always
Indicator 2	1	2	3	4	5

I recognize the importance of boundaries and am able to stay connected to others while at the same time maintaining a sense of self and individuality.

Indicator 3	1	2	3	4	5

I have positive feelings regarding myself and am thus able to create positive feelings in staff.

Indicator 4	1	2	3	4	5

I am willing to take risks but recognize that mistakes and failures are part of the learning process.

Indicator 5	1	2	3	4	5

I am able to acknowledge and learn from my successes as well as my failures.

Indicator 6	1	2	3	4	5

I am able to give and receive both compliments and constructive criticism to and from staff.

Indicator 7	1	2	3	4	5

I make realistic promises and commitments to staff and am able to keep them.

Indicator 8	1	2	3	4	5

I genuinely respect the ideas and feelings of others.

Indicator 9	1	2	3	4	5

I am willing to compromise and negotiate with staff and others in good faith.

| **Indicator 10** | 1 | 2 | 3 | 4 | 5 |

I am capable of saying no and sticking to a position, but I do not need to have my own way at all costs.

| **Indicator 11** | 1 | 2 | 3 | 4 | 5 |

I can handle anger, hostility, put-downs, and lies from staff without undue distress, recognizing that I am defined from within.

| **Indicator 12** | 1 | 2 | 3 | 4 | 5 |

I can handle anger, hostility, put-downs, and lies from staff without responding in kind.

| **Indicator 13** | 1 | 2 | 3 | 4 | 5 |

I am aware of my personal emotions (e.g., anger, anxiety), can name them, and manage them in myself.

| **Indicator 14** | 1 | 2 | 3 | 4 | 5 |

I am prepared for and can cope with the pain that is a normal part of leading a school.

Application

Use this instrument to self-assess your level of assertiveness. The instrument can be used as a self-reflection exercise for a small group of administrators as well as a teaching tool for aspiring principals.

Administration Directions

Circle the number (1–5) that corresponds to the chosen rating (*Never, Seldom, Sometimes, Usually, and Always*) for each indicator.

Scoring Directions

Add up the total points for the fourteen indicators and compute an average score for the overall assessment. For example, if your overall average for the fourteen items is 4.1, you have a high level of assertiveness, with room for growth. *Assertiveness* (as described in Chapter 1) is an overall mindset that is critical for dealing with difficult teachers. The more assertive you are, the more readily and effectively you will be able to increase the productivity and satisfaction of all teachers but especially those who fall into the categories of angry, troubled, exhausted, or just plain confused. If your overall average for the fourteen items is 2.4, you have difficulty asserting yourself, are somewhat conflicted about your role as a principal, and seldom do the "tough" things that assertive principals routinely do.

Time Required

Fifteen minutes to complete the scale

If used by small groups as a reflective exercise, discussion time varies according to the size of the group

The Ten Traits Assessment

Description

The Ten Traits Assessment, Form B.2 (West, 2004), is a scale based on the ten traits of highly effective principals (McEwan, 2003). Staff members are asked to evaluate the principal's progress toward attaining each of the ten traits according to a 4-point rubric: (1) emerging, (2) developing, (3) moving towards mastery, and (4) practicing on a proficient level. An area for explanatory comments is also provided.

Application

Use the form as a way of gathering feedback from staff members relative to your progress toward attaining the ten traits. Cathie West developed the instrument after reading *The Ten Traits of Highly Effective Principals* (McEwan, 2003) and uses it both as a self-assessment and as a way to gather feedback from her staff. She compares her self-ratings on each trait with the overall average rating given by her teachers and sets personal goals based on the findings.

Form B.2   Principal Feedback Form: Ten Traits of Highly
Effective Principals

Emerging	*Developing*	*Moving Toward Mastery*	*Proficient*
1	2	3	4

1. Communicator: a genuine and open human being with the capacity to listen, empathize, interact, and connect with individual students, parents, and teachers in productive, helping, and healing ways, as well as the ability to teach, present, and motivate people in larger group settings

1	2	3	4

2. Educator: a self-directed instructional leader with a strong intellect and personal depth of knowledge regarding research-based curriculum, instruction, and learning that motivates and facilitates the intellectual growth and development of self, students, teachers, and parents

1	2	3	4

3. Envisioner: an individual who is motivated by a sense of calling and purpose, focused on a vision of what schools can be, and guided by a mission that has the best interests of all students at its core

1	2	3	4

4. Facilitator: a leader with outstanding human relations skills that include the abilities to build individual relationships with parents, teachers, and students; collaborative teams with teachers and parents; and a schoolwide community of leaders

1	2	3	4

5. Change Master: a flexible, futuristic, and realistic leader who is able to both motivate and manage change in an organized, positive, and enduring fashion

1	2	3	4

6. Culture Builder: an individual who communicates (talks) and models (walks) a strong and viable vision based on achievement, expectations, character, personal responsibility, and accountability

(Continued)

Form B.2 (Continued)

| 1 | 2 | 3 | 4 |

7. Activator: an individual with gumption (e.g., drive, motivation, enthusiasm, energy, spunk, and humor) enough to spare and share with staff, parents, and students

| 1 | 2 | 3 | 4 |

8. Producer: a results-oriented individual with a strong sense of accountability to taxpayers, parents, students, and teachers who translates high expectations into intellectual development and academic achievement for all students

| 1 | 2 | 3 | 4 |

9. Character Builder: a role model whose values, words, and deeds are marked by trustworthiness, integrity, authenticity, respect, generosity, and humility

| 1 | 2 | 3 | 4 |

10. Contributor: a servant-leader, encourager, and enabler whose utmost priority is making a contribution to the success of others

---

Administration Directions

Give one feedback form to each individual from whom you desire input. Ask staff members to return the forms anonymously to a designated individual who will then collate the results, which are then shared with you.

Scoring Directions

Add up the total from all staff members for each trait. Then compute an average score for each of the ten traits.

Time Required

Fifteen minutes to complete the scale

Time needed to collate responses and compute averages vary according to the number of respondents

The Healthy School Checklist

Description

The Healthy School Checklist, Form B.3.1, contains sixteen indicators that describe aspects of a healthy school culture. Each indicator is followed by five descriptors that define a range of behaviors rated from 1–5.

Form B.3.1 FN   The Healthy School Checklist

Write the number of the Descriptor that best describes an Indicator on the line in front of the Indicator on The Healthy School Checklist Scoring Form.

Indicator 1: All students are treated with respect by all staff members (principal, teachers, instructional aides, secretary and office staff, custodial staff, bus drivers, and cafeteria workers).

Scale of Descriptors:

1. There is an overall feeling on the part of most staff members that students are out of control. Some staff members resort to yelling, "getting physical," sarcasm, and meaningless punishments. There are frequent power struggles between students and adult staff members. Staff members tend to demean students by ignoring problems. Staff members frequently complain about student behavior, a favorite topic of discussion in the teachers' lounge.

2. Although some staff members genuinely respect students and are proactive with regard to troublesome student behavior, they are in the minority. Most teachers feel powerless to change student behavior and treat students with a critical and mean-spirited attitude.

3. Many staff members behave positively and respectfully toward students but are reluctant to defend students or offer positive solutions in the face of their more pessimistic colleagues.

(Continued)

Form B.3.1 FN (Continued)

4. Although most staff members behave positively and respectfully toward students, there are several pockets of resistance and negativism on the part of teachers.

5. All staff members feel positively and act respectfully toward all students, even those who are challenging. When difficulties arise, they handle them through appropriate channels (e.g., Teacher Assistance Team, referral, consultation with principal, etc.).

Indicator 2: The principal and staff establish high expectations for student achievement, which are directly communicated to students and parents.

Scale of Descriptors:

1. Principal and staff believe that nonalterable variables, such as home background, socioeconomic status, and ability level, are the prime determinants of student achievement and that the school cannot overcome these factors.

2. Principal and staff believe that the nonalterable variables cited in Descriptor 1 significantly affect student achievement and that the school has a limited impact on student achievement.

3. Principal and staff believe that although the nonalterable variables cited earlier may influence student achievement, teachers are responsible for all students mastering basic skills or prescribed learner outcomes according to individual levels of expectancy. The principal occasionally communicates these expectations in an informal way to teachers, parents, and students via written and spoken communications, specific activities, or a combination of these.

4. Principal and staff believe that although the nonalterable variables cited earlier may influence student achievement, teachers are responsible for all students mastering certain basic skills at their grade level and frequently communicate these expectations to parents and students in a formal, organized manner. Expectations for student achievement may be communicated through written statements of objectives in basic skills, written statements of purpose or mission for the school that guides the instructional program, or both.

5. Principal and staff believe that together the home and school can have a profound influence on student achievement.

Teachers are held responsible not only for all students mastering certain basic skills at their grade levels but also for the stimulation, enrichment, and acceleration of the students who are able to learn more quickly and the provision of extended learning opportunities for students who may need more time for mastery. Expectations for student achievement are developed jointly among parents, students, and teachers and are communicated through written statements of learner outcomes in core curriculum areas and in enriched and accelerated programs, achievement awards, and opportunities for creative expression.

Indicator 3: The principal and staff members serve as advocates of students and communicate with them regarding aspects of their school life. Behaviors might include lunch with individual students or groups; frequent appearances on the playground, in the lunchroom, and in the hallways; sponsorship of clubs; availability to students who wish to discuss instructional or disciplinary concerns; knowledge of students' names (other than just their own classes) and family relationships; addressing the majority of students by name; and willingness to listen to the students' side in faculty-student problems. The preceding list is meant only to be suggestive of the type of behaviors that might be appropriate for consideration in this category.

Scale of Descriptors:

1. Principal and staff do not feel that acting as student advocates is an appropriate role and never interact with students on this basis.

2. Principal and staff feel that acting as student advocates is an appropriate role but feel uncomfortable and rarely do it. They seldom interact with students on this basis.

3. Principal and staff rarely act as student advocates but engage in at least three behaviors that encourage communication.

4. Principal and staff feel that acting as student advocates is an appropriate role and engage in at least six behaviors that encourage communication.

5. Principal and staff feel that acting as student advocates is an appropriate role and engage in at least six behaviors that encourage communication and establish some means of receiving input from students regarding their opinions of school and classroom life.

(Continued)

Form B.3.1 FN (Continued)

Indicator 4: The principal encourages open communication among staff members and parents and maintains respect for differences of opinion. The main focus of this indicator is on the behaviors that the principal exhibits that give evidence of maintenance of open communication among staff members and parents and maintains respect for differences of opinion. Behaviors might include an open-door policy in the principal's office, acceptance of unpopular ideas and negative feedback from staff and parents, provision of channels for staff and parents to voice grievances or discuss problems, and provision of channels for staff members and parents to interact with each other. The preceding list is meant only to be suggestive of the type of behaviors that might be appropriate for consideration in this category.

Scale of Descriptors:

1. Principal does not encourage open communication among staff members and parents and considers differences of opinion to be a sign of disharmony among organizational members.

2. Principal supports open communication but is rarely available for informal encounters with staff members or parents. Appointments must be scheduled, meeting agendas are tightly maintained, and the flow of information and opinions is artificially controlled.

3. Principal supports open communication and is available for informal encounters with staff members and parents. Principal is not responsive, however, to problems, questions, or disagreements and shuts off communication of this nature.

4. Principal supports open communication and is available for informal encounters with staff members and parents. Principal is responsive to problems, questions, or disagreements and encourages staff members and parents to work through differences of opinion in positive ways.

5. Principal supports open communication and is available for informal encounters with staff members and parents. An open-door policy exists with regard to all problems, questions, and disagreements. Principal structures a variety of opportunities for staff members and parents to interact both formally and informally, encouraging interaction among grade levels, departments, and instructional teams.

Indicator 5: The principal demonstrates concern and openness in the consideration of teacher, parent, or student problems and participates in the resolution of such problems where appropriate.

Scale of Descriptors:

1. Principal does not wish to be involved in the consideration of teacher, parent, or student problems.

2. Principal is willing to be involved in the consideration of teacher, parent, or student problems but is largely ineffective because of poor communication and human relations skills.

3. Principal is willing to be involved in the consideration of teacher, parent, or student problems and is sometimes effective in bringing problems to resolution. Exhibits average communication and human relations skills.

4. Principal is willing to be involved in the consideration of teacher, parent, or student problems and is usually effective in bringing problems to resolution. Exhibits excellent communication and human relations skills.

5. Principal is willing to be involved in the consideration of teacher, parent, or student problems and is nearly always effective in bringing problems to resolution. Exhibits outstanding communication and human relations skills. Has established procedures jointly with faculty for the resolution of problems.

Indicator 6: The principal models appropriate human relations skills. The main focus of this indicator is the variety of appropriate human relations skills that are exhibited by the principal. Behaviors must include, but not necessarily be limited to, (a) establishing a climate of trust and security for students and staff; (b) respecting the rights of students, parents, and staff; (c) handling individual relationships tactfully and with understanding; and (d) accepting the dignity and worth of individuals without regard to appearance, race, creed, sex, disability, ability, or social status.

Scale of Descriptors:

1. Principal exhibits none of the behaviors described.

2. Principal exhibits only one or two of the behaviors described and often has difficulty with tasks that involve human interaction.

(Continued)

Form B.3.1 FN (Continued)

---

3. Principal exhibits two or three of the behaviors described and is usually successful with tasks that involve human interaction.

4. Principal exhibits three or four of the behaviors described and is frequently successful with tasks that involve human interaction.

5. Principal exhibits all of the behaviors described as well as many other behaviors associated with good human relations and is almost always successful with tasks that involve human interaction.

Indicator 7: The principal develops and maintains high morale. The main focus of this indicator is the variety of behaviors exhibited by the principal that contribute to the development and maintenance of high morale. Behaviors might include but are not necessarily limited to involvement of staff in planning, encouragement of planned social events, openness in the dissemination of information, equity in the division of responsibility and allocation of resources, opportunities for achievement, recognition for achievements, involvement of the staff in problem solving, and assistance and support with personal and professional problems.

Scale of Descriptors:

1. Morale is nonexistent in the school building. Principal exhibits none of the behaviors described. There is little unity among staff members, leading to competition, clique formation, destructive criticism, disagreement, and verbal quarreling.

2. Morale is marginal in the school building. Principal exhibits few of the behaviors described. Although fewer visible signs of disunity are evident, faculty members nevertheless do not work well together or have positive feelings about their work.

3. Morale is average. Although there are no visible signs of disunity as seen in Descriptor 1, teachers work largely as individuals, rarely working together cooperatively with enthusiasm and positive feelings.

4. Morale is excellent. Morale-building behaviors by the principal result in teachers working together to share ideas and resources, identify instructional problems, define mutual goals, and coordinate their activities.

5. Morale is outstanding. Morale-building behaviors by the principal result in teachers working together in a highly effective way

while gaining personal satisfaction from their work. Principal has identified specific activities that build morale and systematically engages in these activities.

Indicator 8: The principal systematically collects and responds to staff, parent, and student concerns. The main focus of this indicator is the responsiveness of the principal to the concerns of staff, parents, and students that have been systematically collected. Examples of vehicles used to collect information might include, but are not necessarily limited to, one-on-one conferences, parent or faculty advisory committees, student councils, suggestion boxes, or quality circles.

Scale of Descriptors:

1. No information is collected from staff, parents, and students. Principal is unresponsive to concerns of these groups.

2. Although information is sporadically collected from groups, principal is largely ineffective in responding to concerns.

3. Information is systematically collected from at least one of the three groups, and the principal is effective in responding to concerns.

4. Information is systematically collected from at least two of the three groups, and the principal is effective in responding to concerns.

5. Information is systematically collected from parents, faculty, and students; principal is effective in responding to concerns; and information is used in planning and implementing change.

Indicator 9: The principal appropriately acknowledges the meaningful achievements of others. The main focus of this indicator is the variety of activities engaged in by the principal that demonstrate the ability to recognize the contributions of staff, students, and parents. Activities might include, but are not necessarily limited to, staff recognition programs, student award assemblies, certificates, congratulatory notes, phone calls, recognition luncheons, and newspaper articles.

Scale of Descriptors:

1. Principal engages in no recognition activities.

2. Principal engages in at least one recognition activity for one of the three groups (staff, parents, students).

Form B.3.1 FN (Continued)

---

3. Principal engages in at least one recognition activity for two of the three groups (staff, parents, students).

4. Principal engages in at least one recognition activity for all three groups (staff, parents, students).

5. In addition to a variety of recognition activities, the principal involves all three groups in recognition activities for one another.

Indicator 10: All staff members, classified and certified, are able to communicate openly with one another and say what they feel.

Scale of Descriptors:

1. Discussion is inhibited and stilted. People are hesitant to lay their true feelings on the table and are afraid of criticism, put-downs, and reprisals.

2. A few self-confident or politically connected people speak openly, but most are reluctant.

3. Many staff members speak openly but usually only after a communication trend has been established.

4. Although most communication is open, there are some topics that are taboo, or select individuals inhibit open communication with what they say or do.

5. Discussion is always free-wheeling and frank. There is no hesitation on the part of all staff members to "tell it like it is," even in high-risk discussions and decision making. Staff members feel free to express their feelings as well as their ideas.

Indicator 11: The individual abilities, knowledge, and experience of all staff members are fully used.

Scale of Descriptors:

1. The staff is controlled by one individual who runs the show.

2. A select and chosen few do all the work.

3. At least half of the staff does something, but the same people are always in charge.

4. A majority of the staff participates by doing something, but no effort is made to share or exchange roles.

5. All staff members are recognized as having gifts and talents that are fully used in accomplishing building goals, and roles are shared and exchanged.

Indicator 12: Conflict between various individuals (teachers, parents, students) is resolved openly and effectively, and there is a genuine feeling of respect for one another among these groups.

Scale of Descriptors:

1. People suppress conflict and pretend it does not exist.

2. People recognize conflict but do not approach its solution directly and positively.

3. People recognize conflict and attempt to resolve it with some success, but they are sometimes clumsy and unskilled in their methodology, resulting in frequent misunderstandings.

4. People recognize conflict and can frequently resolve it through appropriate methods, but there are no standardized methodologies for handling conflict.

5. People are skilled at recognizing conflict and have a variety of conflict-resolution strategies in their repertoire that they use with great success.

Indicator 13: The entire school community can articulate and is committed to the vision and mission of the school.

Scale of Descriptors:

1. People are openly committed to their own agendas and are unwilling to set aside personal goals for the school mission.

2. People pretend to be committed to the mission but frequently work at cross-purposes to it.

3. A core of people (staff and parents) is committed, but a few naysayers and bystanders often work to undermine the mission when it serves their purposes.

4. The majority of people are committed, but no intentional efforts have been made to work through any existing group differences.

5. People have worked through their differences, and they can honestly say they are committed to achieving the mission of the school.

(Continued)

Form B.3.1 FN (Continued)

Indicator 14: Staff members can express their views openly without fear of ridicule or retaliation and let others do the same.

Scale of Descriptors:

1. Staff members never express views openly.

2. Some staff members express views openly, but it is usually done with hesitancy and reluctance.

3. Some staff members feel free to express views openly, but many members are reluctant to express their true feelings.

4. Constructive criticism is accepted, but there are no mechanisms for ensuring that it is a regular aspect of teamwork.

5. Constructive criticism is frequent, frank, and two-way; staff members accept and encourage it. Group processes are used that intentionally monitor and encourage the free flow of opinions, ideas, and suggestions for improvement.

Indicator 15: Staff members can get help from one another and can give help without being concerned about hidden agendas.

Scale of Descriptors:

1. Staff members are reluctant to admit ignorance or the need for assistance. They are in the "independent" rather than "interdependent" modes.

2. Some staff members will admit to the need for assistance, but many are territorial and competitive.

3. Staff members want to be cooperative but lack the necessary skills.

4. Staff members assist each other, but there is no systematic plan for evaluating the effectiveness of the cooperative atmosphere.

5. Staff members have no reluctance in asking for help from others or in offering help to fellow staff members. There is transparency and trust among staff members. Processes are used regularly to examine how well the staff is working together and what may be interfering with its cooperation.

Indicator 16: The school climate is characterized by openness and respect for individual differences.

Scale of Descriptors:

1. Parents and staff members are suspicious and disrespectful of one another.

2. A few parents and staff members are trying to improve the climate but are having a difficult time bringing about change.

3. The majority of parents and teachers work well together, but there are some who attempt to undermine a healthy climate.

4. Parents and staff work well together, but little is done to encourage, develop, and affirm this sense of teamwork.

5. Parents and staff respect and affirm the unique gifts and talents of each individual with appreciation for the variety of learning styles, personalities, and intelligences.

Application

Use the Healthy School Checklist yearly or when morale dips, to assess the relative health of your school's culture and determine precisely where the problems may be. The instrument is appropriate for use by small and large groups.

Administration Directions

1. Give each individual who will complete the checklist copies of Form B.3.1, The Healthy School Checklist, and Form B.3.2, The Healthy School Checklist Scoring Form.

2. Read the following instructions to participants: "Read each indicator followed by its scale of five descriptors. Choose the one descriptor that best describes our school and write its number on the line in front of the indicator on The Healthy School Checklist Scoring Form."

Form B.3.2   The Healthy School Checklist Scoring Form

_____ Indicator 1: All students are treated with respect by all staff members (principal, teachers, instructional aides, secretary and office staff, custodial staff, bus drivers, and cafeteria workers).

_____ Indicator 2: The principal and staff establish high expectations for student achievement, which are directly communicated to students and parents.

_____ Indicator 3: The principal and staff members serve as advocates of students and communicate with them regarding aspects of their school life.

_____ Indicator 4: The principal encourages open communication among staff members and parents and maintains respect for differences of opinion.

_____ Indicator 5: The principal demonstrates concern and openness in the consideration of teacher, parent, or student problems and participates in the resolution of such problems where appropriate.

_____ Indicator 6: The principal models appropriate human relations skills.

_____ Indicator 7: The principal develops and maintains high morale.

_____ Indicator 8: The principal systematically collects and responds to staff, parent, and student concerns.

_____ Indicator 9: The principal appropriately acknowledges the meaningful achievements of others.

_____ Indicator 10: All staff members, classified and certified, are able to communicate openly with one another and say what they feel.

_____ Indicator 11: The individual abilities, knowledge, and experience of all staff members are fully used.

_____ Indicator 12: Conflict between various individuals (teachers, parents, students) is resolved openly and effectively, and there is a genuine feeling of respect for one another among these groups.

_____ Indicator 13: The entire school community can articulate and is committed to the vision and mission of the school.

_____ Indicator 14: Staff members can express their views openly without fear of ridicule or retaliation and can permit others to do the same.

_____ Indicator 15: Staff members can get help from one another and can give help without being concerned about hidden agendas.

_____ Indicator 16: The school climate is characterized by openness and respect for individual differences.

_____ Total Score

The checklist can be used in its entirety or you can select individual items to elicit information on specific areas of your school's health. Now take a look at Form 3.3, The Healthy School Checklist Rating Scale.

Scoring Directions

There are two ways to score a *group* of checklists: (1) compute an *overall average rating on the checklist* by adding the individual scores of all respondents and then dividing that total by the number of respondents, or (2) compute *the average scores on individual indicators on the checklist* by adding up the scores of all of the respondents to an individual indicator and then dividing that total by the number of respondents.

Computing an Overall Average Rating

To obtain an overall average rating for all participants, sum the total individual scores for each participant and then compute an average for the entire group. For example, if the ten members of the School Improvement Team completed The Healthy School Checklist and their ratings totaled 636 (67, 74, 62, 57, 71, 59, 68, 42, 79, 57), you would divide this total by 10 to compute the average overall rating—63.6. Then, find that score and its description on the

Form B.3.3 The Healthy School Checklist Rating Scale

Score	Rating
71–80	Superior health: Continue to do all of the effective things you are doing, and regularly monitor the vital signs of your school.
61–70	Excellent health: Even though your school is in great shape, there are a number of actions and behaviors that could notch up its health to Superior.
51–60	Good health: With some fine-tuning in several areas, your school could be much healthier than it is.
41–50	Poor health: One more crisis and your school's health will be failing. Change your lifestyle.
40 and Under	Intensive care! No visitors until further notice!

rating scale. In this example, the team rated the school as being in excellent health.

Computing Average Scores from Selected Items

If input from participants is desired on selected items, individual scores are averaged one indicator at a time. To compute the overall average score for a specific indicator, add up the scores of all of the respondents to that indicator and divide by the total number of respondents. For example, ten faculty members were selected at random and asked to choose the most accurate descriptor for Indicator 4 ("Principal encourages open communication among staff members and parents and maintains respect for differences of opinion."). Their scores were 2, 4, 1, 3, 5, 4, 3, 2, 2, and 1 for a total of 27 and an average of 2.7. This score indicates that a random sample of the faculty feels that the principal needs to open up the flow of communication and be more visible and available to staff members.

The Team Behavior Checklist

Description

The Team Behavior Checklist (Form B.4.1) is a set of indicators describing eight specific aspects of team behavior. Each indicator is followed by five descriptors assigned point values from 1 to 5. The total point value of all eight gives a numerical value to the overall effectiveness of the team's behavior.

Form B.4.1   The Team Behavior Checklist

For each indicator, choose the descriptor that best describes staff behavior. Then record the descriptor's number on the line beside the indicator on The Team Behavior Checklist Scoring Form.

Indicator 1: Team members are able to communicate openly with one another and say what they feel.

Scale of Descriptors:

1. Discussion is inhibited and stilted. Team members hesitate to lay their true feelings on the table and are afraid of criticism, put-downs, and reprisals.

2. A few self-confident or politically connected team members speak openly, but most members are reluctant.

3. Many team members speak openly but usually only after a communication trend has been established.

4. Although most communication is open, there are some topics which are taboo or select individuals who inhibit open communication with what they say or do.

5. Discussion is always freewheeling and frank. There is no hesitation on the part of all team members to "tell it like it is," even in high-risk discussions and decision making. Team members feel free to express their feelings as well as their ideas.

(Continued)

Form B.4.1 (Continued)

Indicator 2: The individual abilities, knowledge, and experience of all team members are fully used.

Scale of Descriptors:

1. The team is controlled by one individual who runs the show.

2. A select and chosen few do all the work.

3. At least half of the members do something, but the same people are always in charge.

4. A majority of the members participate, but no effort is made to share or exchange roles.

5. All team members are recognized as having gifts and talents that are fully used in accomplishing team goals, and roles are shared and exchanged. Whoever is acting as chairperson does not dominate.

Indicator 3: Conflict is resolved openly and effectively.

Scale of Descriptors:

1. Team members suppress conflict and pretend it does not exist.

2. Team members recognize conflict but do not approach its solution directly and positively.

3. Team members recognize conflict and attempt to resolve it with some success, but they are sometimes clumsy and unskilled in their methodology, resulting in frequent misunderstandings.

4. Team members recognize conflict and can frequently resolve it through appropriate methods, but there are no standardized methodologies for handling conflict.

5. Team members are skilled at recognizing conflict and have a variety of conflict resolution strategies in their repertoire that they use with great success.

Indicator 4: Team members are committed to the vision and mission of the team.

Scale of Descriptors:

1. Team members are openly committed to their own agendas and are unwilling to set aside personal goals for the team objective.

2. Team members pretend to be committed to the team objectives but frequently work at cross-purposes to them.

3. A core of team members is committed, but a few naysayers and bystanders work to undermine the team's objectives when it serves their purposes.

4. The majority of team members are committed, but no intentional efforts have been made to work through any existing group differences.

5. Team members have worked through their differences, and they can honestly say they are committed to achieving the objectives of the team. Team processes are in place to assist members in accomplishing this goal.

Indicator 5: Team members can state their views openly without fear of ridicule or retaliation and can let others do the same.

Scale of Descriptors:

1. Team members never express views openly.

2. Team members sometimes express views openly, but it is usually done with hesitancy and reluctance.

3. Some team members feel free to express views openly, but many members are reluctant to express their true feelings.

4. Constructive criticism is accepted, but there are no mechanisms for ensuring that it is a regular aspect of teamwork.

5. Constructive criticism is frequent and frank; team members accept and encourage it. Group processes are used that intentionally monitor and encourage the free flow of opinions, ideas, and suggestions for improvement.

Indicator 6: Everyone accepts responsibility for keeping communication relevant and the team operation on track.

Scale of Descriptors:

1. Meetings are usually disorganized and frequently off task. Agendas are poorly constructed or exist only in the mind of a single individual.

(Continued)

Form B.4.1 (Continued)

2. One or two individuals consistently undermine the effectiveness of team meetings by going off on tangents, making side comments, and demonstrating inappropriate nonverbal language.

3. Meetings are run with an agenda and structure, but time limits are not monitored, and little of worth is accomplished.

4. Most team members accept accountability for the group's behavior, but the accomplishment of tasks is inconsistent.

5. Team members monitor one another's behavior, and all members take responsibility for the effectiveness of team meetings. Agenda items are routinely cared for, and team business is accomplished effectively.

Indicator 7: Team members can get help from others on the team and can give help without being concerned about hidden agendas.

Scale of Descriptors:

1. Team members are reluctant to admit ignorance or the need for assistance. People are in the independent rather than the interdependent mode.

2. Some team members will admit to the need for assistance, but many are territorial and competitive.

3. Team members want to be cooperative but lack the necessary skills.

4. Team members assist each other, but there is no systematic plan for evaluating the effectiveness of the cooperative atmosphere.

5. Team members have no reluctance in asking for help from others or in offering help to fellow members. There is transparency and trust between team members. Processes are used regularly to examine how well the team is working together and what may be interfering with its cooperation.

Indicator 8: The team climate is one of openness and respect for individual differences.

Scale of Descriptors:

1. Team members are suspicious, competitive, and disrespectful.

2. A few team members are trying to improve the climate but are having a difficult time bringing about change.

3. The majority of team members work well together, but there are some who attempt to undermine a healthy climate.

4. The team works well together, but little is done to encourage, develop, and affirm this sense of teamwork.

5. Team members respect and affirm the unique gifts and talents of each member with appreciation for the variety of approaches to problem solving. The team takes time for team-building exercises that improve the climate.

Application

Use this instrument to do a quick assessment of a particular team's effectiveness (e.g., grade level or building leadership) or of the teamwork skills of your entire faculty. The instrument is also helpful for training new team members. The questions examine personal feelings of team (or faculty) members in a way that some other scales do not.

Time Required

Fifteen minutes to complete the scale

Thirty minutes to process the results

Administration Directions

1. Distribute copies of Form B.4.1, The Team Behavior Checklist and B.4.2, The Team Behavior Checklist Scoring Form, to all participants and allow time for completion.

2. Unless you expect group members to share their scores publicly, collect the completed checklists and process the information at another time.

From B.4.3, The Team Behavior Rating Scale, helps you collate the answers you have collected.

Form B.4.2 The Team Behavior Checklist Scoring Form

_____ Indicator 1: Team members are able to communicate openly with one another and say what they feel.

_____ Indicator 2: The individual abilities, knowledge, and experience of all team members are fully used.

_____ Indicator 3: Conflict is resolved openly and effectively.

_____ Indicator 4: Team members are committed to the vision and mission of the team.

_____ Indicator 5: Team members can state their views openly without fear of ridicule or retaliation and can let others do the same.

_____ Indicator 6: Everyone accepts responsibility for keeping communication relevant and the team operation on track.

_____ Indicator 7: Team members can get help from others on the team and can give help without being concerned about hidden agendas.

_____ Indicator 8: The team climate is one of openness and respect for individual differences.

_____ Total Score

Scoring Directions

There are two ways to score a *group* of checklists completed by a team of faculty: (1) compute an *overall average rating on the checklist* by adding the individual scores of all respondents and then dividing that total by the number of respondents, or (2) compute *the average scores on individual indicators on the checklist* by adding up the scores of all of the respondents to that indicator and then dividing that total by the number of respondents.

Form B.4.3   The Team Behavior Rating Scale

Score	Rating
31–40	Mature, effective team: Continue to do all of the positive and productive things you are doing, and regularly monitor your team skills.
20–30	Good team: Even though your team gets the job done, there are some problem relationships that if confronted could notch up your performance to the next level.
10–19	Borderline team: Your team is ignoring the "elephants" that are standing in the way of productivity. Tell it like it is!
Under 10	Dysfunctional team: One more crisis and your team will self-destruct. Do some team-building exercises and put your problems on the table.

Computing an Overall Average Rating

To obtain an overall average rating for all participants, sum the total individual scores for each participant and then compute an average for the entire group. For example, if ten School Improvement Team members completed The Team Behavior Checklist and their individual totals for the checklist were 24, 17, 9, 31, 25, 22, 8, 14, 21, and 22, their average score would be 191 divided by 10, or 19. According to Form B.4.3, the rating scale, this score indicates a borderline team that needs to address issues of trust and communication.

Computing Average Scores From Selected Items

If input from participants is desired on selected items, individual scores are averaged one indicator at a time. To compute the overall average score for a specific indicator, add up the scores of all of the respondents to that indicator and divide by the total number of respondents. For example, information is desired for Indicator 4 ("Team members are committed to the vision and mission of the team."). The scores given by team members were 2, 4, 1, 3, 5, 4, 3, 2, 2, and 1 for a total of 27 and an average of 2.7. This score indicates that although most of the team is committed to its mission and vision, some team-building work is necessary to get everyone on board and working together.

PART 2: GROUP PROCESS EXERCISES

One of the most important aspects of culture building in schools is the effective use of group process exercises. A *process* is an activity or structure that facilitates discussion, guides decision making, and elicits multiple or conflicting viewpoints. Engaging in the process can often be as important for the group as whatever product is produced together (e.g., a mission statement, code of ethics, or set of behavioral expectations for students). Culture builders, rather than being experts with all of the answers, are process experts. There are four things process experts do:

- Help your group to ask the right questions
- Help your group to discuss and debate ideas openly and freely
- Help to create a climate in which your group can make judgments and choice
- Help your group to commit to the decision of their choice

Six processes follow. Choose the group process that satisfies the demands of the task, the characteristics of your group, and your own personal leadership abilities. Doing process activities with a new staff is always a challenge, even if you have already used the process with another group. Leading even a familiar and accepting group through a new and untried process is like teaching a lesson for the first time.

The Code of Ethics Process

Description

This process is designed to develop a staff code of ethics (C. West, 2004). A code of ethics contains "the rules or standards governing the conduct of a person or the conduct of the members of a profession"—in this case, teaching (*The American Heritage Dictionary of the English Language*, 2000).

Application

Use this process to create, nurture, and monitor positive and professional staff behaviors and attitudes.

Time Required

Sixty to ninety minutes

Materials

Many photocopies of the Sample Staff Code of Ethics, Figure B.1, as you will have groups of five to eight individuals

Cut apart each photocopied set of pages into strips and place them into an envelope; you should have as many envelopes as you have groups, each one containing separate strips of all of the statements from the sample code of ethics.

Administration Directions

1. Count off by five (or up to eight). Choose a facilitator (e.g., the person with most years of teaching experience) and a recorder (e. g., the person with the smallest pet).

2. Give the following directions to participants:

   a. Take the enclosed strips of paper from the envelope. Each strip has a different behavioral expectation written on it. One by one, read and discuss each expectation.

   b. Ask the question, Do we want this expectation to be a part of our Code of Ethics?

    c. If your group accepts the statement as it is written, tape it on the chart paper provided.

    d. If your group wants to revise or edit the statement, do that *before* you tape it on the paper.

    e. If you don't want the statement as part of your Code, lay it aside in a separate pile.

    f. Review the list that you have created. Are there any revisions that you want to make or behavior expectations that you want to add?

    g. Record your ideas.

    h. As you consider the statements you have reviewed, which ones were most important to your group? Your recorder should be prepared to share at least one at the conclusion of this exercise.

    i. Turn your work into me, and I will compile your recommendations and submit them to you for final approval.

The Norms of School Culture Process

Description

This process accomplishes three purposes: (1) it assesses how your staff members feel about a specific cultural norm in your school, (2) it elicits their ideas about what the norm should look like in the "ideal" school, and (3) it changes unhealthy cultural norms.

Application

When you encounter dissension, hostility, low expectations, and lack of vision among faculty members, use this process to determine where strengths and problems lie. For example, if your staff members are complaining about their lack of time and energy, choose the norm that focuses on the protection of what's important and work specifically to determine in what ways this norm needs to change.

Figure B.1 Sample Staff Code of Ethics

Mountain Way Elementary School

STAFF CODE OF ETHICS

Cathie West, Principal

The Mountain Way Elementary School Staff will build and maintain respectful, cooperative, and professional relationships by exhibiting the following attitudes and behaviors.

INTERPERSONAL RELATIONS

Speaking positively about each other and remaining loyal to our school family

Trusting and respecting each other and accommodating diverse personalities, teaching styles, and opinions

Recognizing that each staff member brings an educational background, professional experience, and compilation of life skills that are unique and valuable to our school

Modeling forgiveness by letting go of past hurts and working actively to build and maintain healthy relationships

Practicing positive decision making through nondivisive strategies, compromise, and respect for different points of view

CLIMATE

Demonstrating that every job is important and that every person deserves recognition and respect

Looking for humor and laughing a lot

PROFESSIONAL GROWTH

Supporting each other's professional growth through such means as mentoring, peer coaching, and collaborative planning

Improving instruction throughout the school by sharing innovative instructional activities, strategies, and materials

COMMUNICATIONS

Increasing communication between individuals and groups of staff members through professional and social activities

Respecting confidentiality in our communications as they pertain to students, parents, and staff

(Continued)

Figure B.1 (Continued)

Using face-to-face communication and conflict resolution strategies, such as giving "I" messages, when concerns arise

Agreeing to disagree when there are differences that can't be resolved

Using conflict-mediation strategies—including the option of using facilitators—to clear up misunderstandings and resolve conflicts

Keeping open lines of communication between individuals and groups of staff members

Being professional in dress, demeanor, actions, and verbal and written communications

DECISION MAKING

Seeking input from pertinent staff members regarding decisions that affect those members or the faculty as a whole (e.g., major curriculum changes)

Using nondivisive strategies to enhance positive decision making (e.g., decision by consensus, surveys, trouble-shooting committees)

Making every effort to reach acceptable compromises and avoiding decisions that divide the staff by giving ample time for discussion so that consensus can be reached

SCHOOL OPERATIONS

Observing schedules and giving advance notice of schedule changes (e.g., arriving on time for events, vacating shared spaces punctually)

Respecting staff members' property (e.g., asking before borrowing; leaving a note when taking items from the office, library, or staff rooms; returning borrowed items in good condition)

Showing consideration for classroom space and noise levels (e.g., keeping music volume down, refraining from interrupting each other's class time, moving students through halls and shared areas quietly, and keeping family members, especially young children, from invading another's work spaces)

SOURCE: Reprinted by permission of Cathie West.

Background Information

Saphier and King (1985) suggest twelve norms of school culture that impact school improvement: collegiality; experimentation; high expectations; trust and confidence; tangible support; reaching out to the knowledge base; appreciation and recognition; caring, celebration, and humor; shared decision making; protection of what's important; traditions; and honest, open communication (p. 67).

Here's how these norms might look in a school with a strong positive culture:

- Collegiality: Staff members are willing to share ideas, solve instructional problems together, and assume joint responsibility for all of the students in the school and their learning.
- Experimentation: Staff members are willing to take risks in learning new techniques, teaming with others, and trying alternative methodologies when what they are using is not working.
- High expectations: The principal, teachers, parents, and students are expected to rise to a stated set of standards in their behavior, attitudes, instruction, and learning.
- Trust and confidence: Administrators, teachers, students, and parents maintain a high level of trust and confidence in one other.
- Tangible support: The principal provides financial, human, and emotional resources to teachers so they can accomplish the mission of the school.
- Reaching out to the knowledge base: Instructional methodologies and curricular materials are chosen and evaluated by using reliable scientific research.
- Appreciation and recognition: Teachers know that what they do is important, praiseworthy, and appreciated in both tangible and intangible ways.
- Caring, celebration, and humor: All members of the school community endeavor to build social connections, taking time for fun and laughter as they work to achieve the mission of the school.
- Involvement in decision making: Teachers are included in meaningful decision-making processes in the school, particularly if those decisions impact teaching and learning.
- Protection of what's important: The principal protects teachers' time and energies so they can maximize teaching and learning.

- Traditions: Members of the school community value and encourage practices and ceremonies that preserve history, honor the heroes and heroines of the school, and keep the best of the past alive.
- Honest, open communication: All members of the school community are able to speak the truth in love to one another with the ultimate goal of helping students to learn and grow.

Process Directions

1. Divide your faculty into small groups of from three to five individuals.

2. Assign one of Saphier and King's norms of school culture to each group. Or if you prefer, choose one norm and assign it to everyone.

3. Use the Norms of School Culture Worksheet, Form B.5, to focus small-group discussions of the assigned norm. Each group should choose a recorder to take notes during the discussion and a reporter to summarize its findings and conclusions for the large group. Use the information to develop school improvement goals.

Force Field Analysis

Description

Force Field Analysis is a problem-solving process developed by Kurt Lewin in the 1940s. Participants identify a problem and then describe the driving forces that push toward a solution of the problem and the restraining forces that work against solving it.

Application

When a situation or problem has been defined or a solution or plan of action has been determined, the force field analysis process encourages group members to verbalize both positive and negative

Form B.5   Norms of School Culture Worksheet

Norm: _____

What practices or conditions in our school currently strengthen this norm?

What practices or conditions in our school weaken this norm?

What would this norm look like at its best?

What specific recommendations do you have to improve this norm?

What would you be willing to do to improve this norm in our school?

feelings about the situation or the proposed solution. Identification of positive forces enables group members to capitalize and strengthen these forces, and verbalization of the negatives illuminates erroneous information and issues that may be hindering the accomplishment of goals. Force field analysis always works best when it involves the group members who are most resistant to change and enlists them in solving the problems.

Time Required

One hour to ninety minutes

Group Size

Five to thirty-five participants

Materials

Chart paper, colored markers, pushpins or masking tape

Copies of Form B. 6, the Force Field Analysis Worksheet, for all participants

Transparency of the Sample Force Field Analysis, Exhibit B.1

Process Directions

1. Put a copy of Form B.6 on an overhead transparency or chart paper. Exhibit B.1 shows a sample analysis for your information or to share with your staff if you choose.

2. Generate a list of facilitating (positive or driving) forces that will help the team to solve the problem. Answer the question, What forces will help us to make the needed change? If a force appears to be complex, break it down into its separate components, if possible. Do not worry at this point about which forces are more important.

3. Then generate a list of restraining (negative) forces that will get in the way of a solution or achievement of a goal— include as many as you can think of. Answer the question, What forces will try to stop change from occurring?

Form B.6   Force Field Analysis Worksheet

Goal:

Facilitating Forces	*Restraining Forces*

Exhibit B.1 Sample Force Field Analysis

Goal: To create and nurture a positive school culture.	
Facilitating Forces	Restraining Forces
⟶	⟵
Dedicated, caring, hardworking, and knowledgeable faculty Resources to provide staff development Core group of high-achieving students and parents	Too many students below grade level when they enroll at our school Staff members who are negative and critical Lack of respect for younger teachers Low expectations regarding what we can realistically accomplish with low-achieving students Discouraged and exhausted teachers Lack of affirmation and praise for our hard work Too much interference from central office

4. Rank the restraining forces, agreeing on two or three that are most important. Rate these for their solvability. Do not waste time focusing on unsolvable problems or "unalterable variables," as they are called by Benjamin Bloom (1980).

5. For each restraining force you have listed as important, describe some possible action steps you might be able to carry out that would reduce the effect of the force or eliminate it completely.

6. Review the action steps you have listed, circle those you intend to do, and move to an action plan immediately—or you may defer that to another meeting.

The Parking Lot Meeting Process

Description

This process legitimatizes a practice that goes on in many schools (particularly in the early days of culture building)— teachers not saying what's really on their minds in a meeting (e.g., sitting silently, avoiding eye contact, appearing uptight) and then going out to the parking lot and saying what they really think.

Application

Use this process whenever you feel a decision-making meeting is going poorly: (a) if the participants are not speaking openly, (b) if the climate is strained, and (c) if people are weighing their words very carefully. A parking-lot meeting process will get the crucial issues on the table and out in the open.

Time Required

Thirty to forty-five minutes

Group Size

Twenty-five to fifty participants

Materials

Chart paper, colored markers, pushpins, and masking tape

Process Directions

1. Use this process either as part of the regular meeting or in a specially called parking-lot meeting.

2. Form participants into parking lot groups of their choice.

3. Describe the concept of parking-lot meetings and give them about fifteen to twenty minutes to conduct their meetings.

4. Convene all groups and ask each parking lot group to share the substance of its discussion with the entire group. Select

a recorder to list on chart paper all of the problems or concerns mentioned.

5. Deal with the issues that were raised and proceed with other consensus decision-making processes.

The Apollo Process

Description

The Apollo Process is a consensus activity that enables a group to synthesize its members' diverse reactions and opinions into a concise list of recommendations. All members of the group have an opportunity to contribute their ideas. As a result, support for the final goal is likely to be more cohesive.

Application

The Apollo Process is useful for synthesizing reactions from your entire faculty regarding a proposal or idea. The small groups give individuals an opportunity to express their opinions freely, without the constraints that often are present in a large group setting. The views of each group can then be synthesized. The ease with which consensus is reached will enable the principal to determine if more process activities are needed.

Time Required

One hour to ninety minutes

Group Size

Ten to forty participants

Materials

Chart paper and colored markers

Process Directions

1. Recommendation(s) are made to the large group.

2. The large group is then randomly divided into groups of three to five members.

3. Members of each group should sit close enough to one another that they can share materials, talk to each other quietly, and maintain eye contact with all other members.

4. Each group member should have a different role assigned by the group. Such roles could include summarizer (restates the group's major conclusions or answers), checker (ensures that all members can explain how the answer or conclusion was determined), and encourager (ensures that all members participate actively in the discussion).

5. The group must collaborate to arrive at one decision or recommendation from the group. Ideally all members should be in agreement, and all members should be able to explain the rationale underlying their decision.

6. Each group makes a presentation of its opinions or ideas to the large group.

The WOTS Up Analysis

Description

The WOTS Up Analysis gets its name from the four words that produce the WOTS acronym: *weaknesses, opportunities, threats, and strengths*. Having a clear understanding of these four aspects of your school will help your leadership team or entire faculty determine the critical problems to be solved.

Application

This process is an easy way to conduct a situation audit regarding the state of a school, using the input from a large group of people (the faculty). The information gathered can then be used by a planning team to problem solve and plan.

Time Required

Fifteen to thirty minutes for individuals to complete Form B.7, the WOTS Up Planning Form, in private

Sixty to ninety minutes for a small leadership group to collate and discuss the findings

Form B.7   WOTS Up Planning Form

What are the major WEAKNESSES of our school?	
What are the major OPPORTUNITIES available to our school?	
What are the major THREATS facing our school?	
What are the major STRENGTHS of our school?	

Group Size

Twenty-five to fifty members to complete the questionnaire

A team of five to ten to collate, discuss, and process the results

Materials

A copy of Form B. 7, the WOTS Up Planning Form, for each participant

Chart paper and colored markers to collate the results

Process Directions

1. Introduce the WOTS Up Planning Form and distribute it in a large group meeting. Explain the reasons you are gathering the information (to help in goal setting for the coming year, to determine the strengths and weaknesses of your school, etc.). Discuss what is meant by the four categories (weaknesses, opportunities, threats, and strengths).

2. Identify three or four trusted members of the group (they may be members of the leadership or school management team) to collect the questionnaires.

3. Meet with the team to collate the results. Determine if there is consensus on the major opportunities, threats, strengths, and weaknesses. If consensus exists, there may be no need to return to the large group until a proposal for seizing opportunities, minimizing threats, maximizing strengths, and strengthening weaknesses has been developed.

4. If after collating the results, there is great divergence, however, then return to the large group and conduct a consensus-building process, such as an Apollo Process, to bring focus to a viable starting point for your efforts to effect change and improvement.

References

Achilles, C., Keedy J., & High, R. (1999). The workaday world of the principal. How principals get things done. In L. Hughes (Ed.), *The principal as leader* (pp. 25-58). New York: Macmillan.

Alleghany County Public Schools. (2004). *Sexual harassment/harassment based on race, national origin, disability and religion policy JFHA/GBA.* Covington, VA: Author.

American Heritage Dictionary of the English Language, 4th Edition. (2000). New York: Houghton Mifflin. Retrieved January 5, 2005 from www.bartleby.com/61/

American Psychiatric Association. (2002). *Diagnostic and Statistical Manual of Mental Disorders* (4th ed., text revision). Washington, DC: American Psychiatric Association.

Andelson, S. J. (2001). *FRISK documentation model: Practical guidelines for evaluators in documenting unsatisfactory employee performance.* Cerritos, CA: Atkinson, Andelson, Loya, Ruud & Romo.

Argyris, C. (1986). Skilled incompetence. *Harvard Business Review, 64,* 74-79.

Argyris, C. (1991). Teaching smart people how to learn. *Harvard Business Review, 69,* 99-109.

Arizona Department of Education. (2003, April). *State of Arizona reporting procedures.* Phoenix: Arizona State Board of Education.

Autry, J. (1991). *Love and profit: The art of caring leadership.* New York: William Morrow.

Axelrod, A., & Holtje, J. (1997). *201 ways to deal with difficult people.* New York: McGraw-Hill.

Bailey, S. (1971). Preparing administrators for conflict resolution. *Educational Record, 53,* 225.

Bellon, J. (1988). The dimensions of leadership. *Vocational Education Journal, 63*(6), 29-31.

Blase, J., & Blase, J. (1998). *Handbook of instructional leadership: How really good principals promote teaching and learning.* Thousand Oaks, CA: Corwin.

Blase, J., & Blase, J. (2003). *Breaking the silence: Overcoming the problem of principal mistreatment of teachers.* Thousand Oaks, CA: Corwin.

Blase, J., & Kirby, P. (2000). *Bringing out the best in teachers.* Thousand Oaks, CA: Corwin.

Bloom, B. S. (1980). The new direction in educational research: Alterable variables. *Phi Delta Kappan, 61,* 382-385.

Brinkman, R., & Kirschner, R. (1994). *Dealing with people you can't stand.* New York: McGraw-Hill.

Brody Communications Ltd. (2004). *Strengthening interpersonal relationships.* Retrieved January 5, 2005, from www.brodycommunications.com

Brown, M. W. (1949). *The important book.* New York: HarperCollins.

Bryk, A., & Schneider, B. (2002). *Trust in schools.* New York: Russell Sage.

Buckingham, M., & Coffman, C. (1999). *First break all the rules: What the world's greatest managers do differently.* New York: Simon & Schuster.

Buckingham, M., & Coffman, C. (2001). *Now, discover your strengths.* New York: Free Press.

Carey, B. (2004, June 22). Fear in the workplace: The bullying boss. *New York Times.* Retrieved January 5, 2005, from http://www.nytimes.com

Clifton, D. O., & Nelson, P. (1992). *Soar with your strengths.* New York: Dell.

Cloud, H., & Townsend, J. (1992). *Boundaries.* Grand Rapids, MI: Zondervan.

Collins, J. (2001). *Good to great: Why some companies make the leap and others don't.* New York: HarperBusiness.

Covey, S. (1989). *7 habits of highly effective people.* New York: Simon & Schuster.

Crowe, S. (1999). *Since strangling isn't an option: Dealing with difficult people— Common problems and uncommon solutions.* New York: Perigree.

DeBono, E. (1999). *Six thinking hats.* Boston: Little, Brown.

Downey, C. J., Steffy, B. E., English, F. E., Frase, L. E., & Poston, W. K. (2004). *The three-minute classroom walk-through: Changing school supervisory practice one teacher at a time.* Thousand Oaks, CA: Corwin.

Drucker, P. (2004). *BrainyQuote.* Retrieved January 5, 2005, from www.brainy quote

DuFour, R. P., & Eaker, R. (1987). *Fulfilling the promise of excellence: A practitioner's guide to school improvement.* Westbury, NY: Wilkerson.

Ehrgott, R. (April, 1992). *A study of the marginal teacher in California.* Paper presented at the annual meeting of the California Educational Research Association, San Francisco. (ERIC Document Reproduction Service No. ED356556)

Farson, R. (1996). *Management of the absurd: Paradoxes in leadership.* New York: Simon & Schuster.

Friedman, E. H. (1991). Bowen theory and therapy. In A. S. Gurman & D. P. Kniskern (Eds.), *Handbook of family therapy* (pp. 134-170). New York: Brunner/Mazel.

Fullan, M. (1991). *The new meaning of educational change.* New York: Teachers College Press.

Fullan, M. (1998). Leadership for the 21st century: Breaking the bonds of dependency. *Educational Leadership, 55*(7), 6-10.

Fullan, M. (2003). *The moral imperative of school leadership.* Thousand Oaks, CA: Corwin.

Goodwin, A. L. (1987). Vocational choice and the realities of teaching. In F. S. Bolin & J. M. Falk (Eds.), *Teacher renewal: Professional issues, personal choice* (pp. 30-36). New York: Teachers College Press.

Gordon, T. (1970). *Parent effectiveness training.* New York: Wyden.

Guralnik, D. B. (Ed.). (1980). *Webster's new world dictionary of the English language.* New York: William Collins.

Hallowell, E. (2004). *Dare to forgive.* Deerfield Beach, FL: Health Communications.

Hankins, G., & Hankins, C. (1988). *Prescription for anger: Coping with angry feelings and angry people.* New York: Warner.

Harris, S. J. (n.d.). Retrieved January 5, 2005, from http://www.worldofquotes.com

Hawley, J. A. (1993). *Reawakening the spirit in work: The power of dharmic management.* San Francisco: Berrett-Koehler.

Heifetz, R., & Linsky, M. (2002). *Leadership on the line: Staying alive through the dangers of leading.* Boston: Harvard Business School Press.

Hersey, P., & Blanchard, K. H. (1977). *Management of organizational behavior: Utilizing human resources.* Englewood Cliffs, NJ: Prentice Hall.

Horn, S. (1996). *Tongue fu! How to deflect, disarm, and defuse any verbal conflict.* New York: St. Martin's Griffin.

Jackson, P. (1968). *Life in classrooms.* New York: Holt, Rinehart & Winston.

Johnson, D. W., & Johnson, R. G. (1989). *Leading the cooperative school.* Edina, MN: Interaction.

Jones, L., & McBride, R. (1990). *An introduction to team-approach problem solving.* Milwaukee, WI: ASQC.

Josephson, M. (2004). *Respect* (Commentary 364.2). Retrieved January 5, 2005, from www.charactercounts.com

Joyce, B., & Showers, J. (1988). *Student achievement through staff development.* New York: Longman.

Kalb, C. (2003, February 24). Coping with anxiety: Science shows that meditation, massage, yoga—even laughter—can change bad habits in the brain. *Newsweek,* pp. 51-52.

Kanter, R. M. (2004). *Confidence: How winning streaks and losing streaks begin and end.* Chicago: Crown.

Keillor, G. (1985). *Lake Wobegon days.* New York: Viking.

Kelly, E. A. (1980). *Improving school climate.* Reston, VA: National Association of Secondary School Principals.

Kingsolver, B. (1995). *High tide in Tucson.* New York: HarperCollins.

Kouzes, J. M., & Posner, B. Z. (1999). *Encouraging the heart: A leader's guide to rewarding and recognizing others.* San Francisco: Jossey-Bass.

Lamott, A. (1994). *Some instructions on writing and life.* New York: Anchor.

Lamperes, B. (2004). 10 strategies for staff development. *Principal Leadership.* Retrieved January 5, 2005, from nasspcms.principals.org

Lao-Tzu. (1988). *Tao te ching: A New English Version.* New York: Harper Perennial. (Original version from the 6th century BCE)

Lawrence, C. E., & Vachon, M. (2003). *How to handle staff misconduct: A practical guide for school principals and supervisors.* Thousand Oaks, CA: Corwin.

Lawrence, C. E., Vachon, M. K., Leake, D. O., & Leake, B. H. (2001). *The marginal teacher: A step-by-step guide to fair procedures for identification and dismissal.* Thousand Oaks, CA: Corwin.

Lebelle, L. (2000). Personality disorders. Retrieved January 5, 2005, www.focusas.com

Little, J. W. (1989, April). *The persistence of privacy: Autonomy and initiative in teachers' professional relations.* Paper presented at the annual meeting of the American Educational Research Association, San Francisco.

Loehr, J., & Schwartz, T. (2003). *The power of full engagement: Managing energy, not time is the key to high performance and personal renewal.* New York: Free Press.

Lynch, R. F., & Werner, T. J. (1992). *Continuous improvement: Teams and tools.* Atlanta, GA: QualTeam.

Markham, U. (1993). *How to deal with difficult people.* London: Element.

McEwan, E. K. (1997). *Leading your team to excellence: How to make quality decisions.* Thousand Oaks, CA: Corwin Press.

McEwan, E. K. (2002a). *Teach them all to read: Catching the kids who fall through the cracks.* Thousand Oaks, CA: Corwin Press.

McEwan, E. K. (2002b). *Ten traits of highly effective teachers: How to hire, coach, and mentor successful teachers.* Thousand Oaks, CA: Corwin.

McEwan, E. K. (2003). *Ten traits of highly effective principals.* Thousand Oaks, CA: Corwin.

McEwan, E. K. (2004). *How to deal with parents who are angry, troubled, afraid, or just plain crazy* (2nd ed.). Thousand Oaks, CA: Corwin.

McGregor, D. (1960). *The human side of enterprise.* New York: McGraw-Hill.

Miller, W. R., & Rollnick, S. R. (2002). *Motivational interviewing: Preparing people for change.* New York: Guilford.

Montgomery, B. (1961). *The path to leadership.* New York: Putnam.

Morales. A. (December 24, 2004). Image protection harms children. *Northwest Explorer.* Retrieved January 5, 2005, from www.explorernews.com

Murphy, C. U., & Lick, D. W. (2001). *Whole-faculty study groups. Creating student-based professional development.* Thousand Oaks, CA: Corwin.

Nanus, B. (1992). *Visionary leadership.* San Francisco: Jossey-Bass.

O'Connor, A. (2004, September 10, 2004). Cracking under pressure? It's just the opposite. *New York Times.* Retrieved January 5, 2005, from www.nytimes.com

Peck, M. S. (1978). *The road less traveled.* New York: Simon & Schuster.

Perkins, D. (1992). *Smart schools: From training memories to educating minds.* New York: Free Press.

Pirsig, R. (1974). *Zen and the art of motorcycle maintenance.* New York: William Morrow.

Pritchett, P., & Pound, R. (1993). *High-velocity culture change: A handbook for managers.* Dallas: Pritchett.

Prochaska, J. O., Norcross, J. C., & Diclemente, C. C. (2002). *Changing for good: A revolutionary six-stage program for overcoming bad habits and moving your life positively forward.* New York: Quill.

Ramsey, R. D. (2003). *School leadership from A to Z: Practical lessons from successful schools and businesses.* Thousand Oaks, CA: Corwin Press.

Rollnick, S., Mason, P., & Butler, C. (1999). *Health behavior change: A guide for practitioners.* Edinburgh, Scotland: Churchill Livingstone.

Rosen, M. I. (1998). *Thank you for being such a pain: Spiritual guidance for dealing with difficult people.* New York: Three Rivers Press.

Saint-Exupéry, A. (1950). *Wisdom of the sands* (S. Gilbert, Trans.). New York: Harcourt Brace.

Saphier, J., & King, M. (1985). Good seeds grow in strong cultures. *Educational Leadership, 43,* 67-74.

Scanlon Leadership Network. (2003). *The courage to test reality.* Retrieved January 5, 2005, from www.scanlonleader.org

Scarpinato, D. (December 2, 2004). Marana school slow to report sexual abuse. *Arizona Daily Star,* G12.

Scearce, C. (1992). *100 ways to build teams.* Palatine, IL: IRI/Skylight.

Schmoker, M. (1999). *Results: The key to continuous school improvement* (2nd ed.). Alexandria, VA: Association for Supervision and Curriculum Development.

Schmoker, M. (2001). *The results fieldbook: Practical strategies from dramatically improved schools.* Alexandria, VA: Association for Supervision and Curriculum Development.

Scott, S. (2002). *Fierce conversations: Achieving success at work and in life, one conversation at a time.* New York: Penguin Viking.

Senge, P. (1990). *The fifth discipline.* Garden City, NY: Doubleday.

Senge, P., Kleiner, A., Roberts, C., Ross, R. B., & Smith, B. J. (Eds.). (1994). *The fifth discipline fieldbook: Strategies and tools for building a learning organization.* Garden City, NY: Doubleday.

Sergiovanni, T. (2000). Leadership as stewardship: Who's serving who? In *The Jossey-Bass reader on educational leadership* (pp. 269-286). San Francisco: Jossey-Bass.

Shinn, L. (2004, January 16–18). You can be a great storyteller. *USA Weekend,* p. 14.

Short, P. M., & Rinehart, J. S. (1992). School participant empowerment scale: Assessment of the level of empowerment within the school environment. *Educational and Psychological Measurement, 52,* 951-960.

Surgeon General of the United States. (1999). *Mental health: A report of the Surgeon General.* Retrieved January 5, 2005, www.surgeongeneral.gov

Tapia, S. T. (July 24, 1997). Ex Marana teacher faces third sexual abuse lawsuit. *Arizona Daily Star,* p. 2B.

Tavris, C. (1978). *Anger: The misunderstood emotion.* New York: Simon & Schuster.

Taylor, G., & Wilson, R. (1997). *Helping angry people: A short-term structured model for pastoral counselors.* Vancouver, British Columbia: Regent College.

Tough Love International. (2004). Retrieved August 11, 2004,

Wegela, K. K. (1996). *How to be a help instead of a nuisance.* Boston: Shambhala.

Weiss, R. P. (2004). *The mind-body connection in learning.* National Institute of Anxiety and Stress. Retrieved January 5, 2005, from www.trans4mind.com

West, C. (2004). *The ten traits assessment.* Unpublished document.

Wildlife Hazards for Campers and Hikers. (2004) Retrieved January 5, 2005, from www.geocities.yahoo.com

Word for Word. (2004). Retrieved January 5, 2005, from www.plateaupress.com

Ziglar, Z. (1986). *Top performance: How to develop excellence in yourself and others.* New York: Berkley Books.

Index

**CORWIN
PRESS**

The Corwin Press logo—a raven striding across an open book—represents the union of courage and learning. Corwin Press is committed to improving education for all learners by publishing books and other professional development resources for those serving the field of K–12 education. By providing practical, hands-on materials, Corwin Press continues to carry out the promise of its motto: **"Helping Educators Do Their Work Better."**